Financial Mathematics

Simplified Handbook for learning and remembering

Cacildo Marques

ISBN: **979-8741574713**

Cover: Abstract art

Episteme Ed

Marques, Cacildo

**Financial Mathematics: Simplified Handbook for learning and
remembering.**/ Maryland, 2021.

154p.

ISBN: **979-8741574713**

1. Mathematics. 2. Financial Mathematics. I. Title

DDC 519.5

Financial Mathematics

Simplified Handbook for learning and remembering

Cacildo Marques

CONTENTS

	Preface	viii
Chapter 0	**Rational numbers and progressions**	11
Chapter 1	**Interest**	44
Chapter 2	**Interest yield time**	55
Chapter 3	**Simple annuities**	79
Chapter 4	**Payments, deadline and interest on annuities**	87
Chapter 5	**Amortization**	97
Chapter 6	**Bonds**	124
APPENDIX	Annuities in Excel - Annuities in HP 12C	132

Preface

Words of demystification and encouragement

Basic education curricular programs do not usually address the theme of Financial Mathematics in a functional way. In the United States there is a concern with the chapter on annuities (periodic payments), but few other countries reproduce this idea. In most countries, the chapter called Financial Mathematics in Mathematics books deals only with interest. And there are also cases of curricula that, when dealing with interest in elementary school II (junior high school), present only the idea of simple interest, not to mention compound interest. This practice leaves a damaging gap in the preparation of students, because whenever we talk about interest, we must first think of compound interest, not simple interest, rarely used in the market.

This book seeks to serve as didactic material to accompany university courses, without complications, but also to deepen the most important points of Financial Mathematics for people graduated from high school, or even those of complete elementary school, since they do not makes use of Higher Mathematics resources.

In addition to not being a difficult content, it is of great use, for professionals in the field and for the citizen in general. Exercising, many exercises, is the secret of learning any subject involving Arithmetic, Geometry and Algebra. So, for those who want to learn, get to work!

Cacildo Marques, S. Paulo, April 2021.

x

Chapter 0 - Rational numbers and progressions

This first chapter is very basic. Whoever is qualified in *percentage* accounts, algebraic sum, arithmetic expressions, fractional numerals and the meaning of these concepts, can turn the pages and study the next chapter directly. The invitation to jump is addressed to those who are in a hurry, because Mathematics is fun, its exercises are amusing games, and those who study all topics can only win.

Whenever possible here, examples and exercises refer to situations of Geometry, which is the visual part of Mathematics.

Relative integers

Taking into account that the student is very familiar with natural numbers, we start with a recall of the relative integers in their basic operations of addition, multiplication and division.

If we say the temperature is 3 degrees below zero, we are considering it to be minus 3 degrees, or -3 degrees. On the number line with the numbers 0, 1, 2, 3, and so on, the negative integers are those that occupy positions symmetrical to those.

$$-3 \quad -2 \quad -1 \quad 0 \quad +1 \quad +2 \quad +3 \quad +4...$$

If we perform (-3) + (+3), sum of -3 and +3, the result is 0, since they are symmetrical, that is, they are at the same distance from zero on the line. If our operation is in addition, represented by the plus sign, "+", between the parentheses, just count the values that are in the parentheses, as is the case there from -3 and +3, in which we discount 3 from +3. If we have several parentheses in the operation, the most convenient technique is to join the values of the "+" sign in one parenthesis and those of the minus sign, "-", in another, to finally make the count with these two.

Thus,

$(-7) + (+2) + (-5) + (-1) + (+9) + (+4) = (+15) + (-13) = +2.$

It doesn't matter if we add $(+15) + (-13)$ or $(-13) + (+15)$. If the negative is before, just check backwards.

If the operation indicated by the sign in parentheses is a subtraction, "-" sign, the simplest process is to transform the account into addition. For example, $(+8) - (+3)$ is the same as $(+8) + (-3)$, and this gives a +5 result. What we did was change the position of the signs before and after opening the parenthesis of +3, because the value -(+3) is the same as +(-3), that is, the symmetrical of +3 is the same as the positive sign applied to -3.

What if we have -(-5)? Now, the symmetric of -5 is the opposite position value on the line, +5. So $-(-5) = +(+5)$.

Doing $(+6) - (-7)$ is the same as doing $(+6) + (+7) = +13$.

While taking the number 1 as a reference, we see that $-(+1) = +(-1) = -1$. And now we also know that $-(-1) = +(+1) = +1$.

We can now eliminate the parentheses of all these addition and subtraction operations.

To do $(-3) + (-4) + (-2) - (-4) + (-8) + (-1) - (-6)$, we write the expression as:

$-3 - 4 - 2 + 4 - 8 - 1 + 6 = + 10 - 18 = -8.$

The operation we did is called *algebraic sum*, in which addition and subtraction operations are treated in the same way, as the sum of relative numbers. (If in the algebraic sum a number starts without its preceding sign, that sign is positive.)

In the following exercises, beginning with P, meaning "proposed", the first item will always be an example, and the following items are left for the reader to solve. The recommendation is that the accounts be made in pencil, leaving the calculator for use in advanced topics, which we will see later, such as those involving powers and non-whole roots. If the calculator is used in simple accounts, it is the one who is learning.

Exercise **P0.01**
Get the result of each algebraic sum below.
A) 4 - 2 + 7 - 8 + 3 − 10.
Resolution:
4 - 2 + 7 - 8 + 3 - 10 = 14 - 20 = -6.
　B) - 2 - 4 - 6 +1 - 12 +7. C) 8 - 1 + 4 + 5 + 3 − 9. D) - 5 - 4 - 7 - 3 + 6 + 2. E) 7 + 2 +8 - 6 -2 - 4.

If we want to multiply two relative numbers, the sign "rule" is the same as for the symmetric one. For example, $(+2)*(-3) = = 2*(-3) = -6$. What if we have $(-1)*(-5)$? This can be written as $-1*(-5)$, or as $-(-5)$, since 1 is the neutral element of multiplication. We can also understand that $(-1)*(-5) = = -(+1)*(-5) = -(-5) = +5$.

All of this is for us to be convinced that $(-1)*(-1) = +1$ and that $(+1)*(-1) = (-1)*(+1) = -1$. If we multiply two numbers of the same sign, the result is positive. If we multiply numbers of opposite signs, the result is negative.

Minus "times" minus is plus; plus "times" minus is minus. Note: We should never say "with" instead of "times" when it comes to multiplication.

As we will see below, the division is the multiplication by the inverse value of the number. So the sign "rule" of division is the same as multiplication. Thus, $(-12): (-3) = +4$.

Exercise **P0.02**
Perform the operations below.
A) $(-7)*(-3)$.
Resolution:
$(-7)*(-3) = +21$.

B) (-4)*(- 8). C) (+3)*(-5). D) (-8)*(-2). E) (-4)*(+7). F) (-15): (+3).

Fractions

Rational numbers are all n/p values, for integer **n** and non-zero integer **p**. They can be represented in form of fraction, as in 4/5, or in form of decimal numbers, as in 0.8.

A number represented as a decimal number can be an exact decimal, such as 1.35, a periodic tithe, such as 2.4444..., or an irrational number, which cannot be expressed as a fraction, this being the case with the number 0.101001000100001..., from the classic example of Richard Courant and Herbert Robbins.

To represent a fraction as a decimal number, just divide the numerator **n** by the denominator **p**. It was done with 4/5 above. Dividing 4 by 5 gives 0.8.

A fraction with a numerator lesser than its denominator is called a *proper fraction*, as is the case with 4/5, and the value will always be less than 1. If the numerator is greater than the denominator, as in 9/4, we have an *improper fraction*, which always has a value greater than 1. When the division of numerator by denominator results in an integer, as in 8/2, which gives 4, we have an *apparent fraction*.

When a fraction that is simplified has in the denominator only factors of the prime numbers 2 and 5, such as 4, 5, 8, 10, 16 and 20, dividing the numerator by denominator produces an exact decimal. In other cases, the result will be a periodic tithe.

A fraction is simplified when there is no more common factor to be cut between numerator and denominator, that is, when the greatest common divisor (GCD, or GCF: greatest common factor) between these two numbers is equal to 1. In the fraction 8/14, the GCD between terms is 2, therefore, we can simplify by 2:

$$\frac{8}{14} = \frac{8:2}{14:2} = \frac{4}{7}$$

In the case of factor 2, just check that the two terms are even numbers, and then simplify the fraction.

If we are going to add fractions that have the same denominator, it is only necessary to add the numerators. For example, 1/8 + 5/8 = 6/8. (This fraction after simplified gives 3/4.)

|■|□|□|□|□|□|□|□|

|■|■|■|■|■|□|□|□|

In most situations, however, the fractions we have to add have different denominators. Then it will be necessary for us to apply a technique that transforms these fractions into equivalent fractions, that is, fractions of the same value, but that have equal denominators.

To obtain a fraction equivalent to a given fraction, it is enough that we multiply numerator and denominator by the same non-zero integer. For example,

$$\frac{3}{4} = \frac{3*5}{4*5} = \frac{15}{20}$$

The fraction 15/20 is equivalent to the irreducible fraction 3/4. (*Irreducible fraction* is the one that is simplified, that is, that has GCD 1 among its terms.)

If we add 7/5 + 3/4, the necessary step is to write this as the sum of fractions of the same denominator. The fraction 3/4, as we already know, has as its equivalent the fraction 15/20. For the fraction 7/5 it is enough that we multiply numerator and denominator by 4:

$$\frac{7}{5} = \frac{7*4}{5*4} = \frac{28}{20}$$

Our sum will be:

$$\frac{7}{5} + \frac{3}{4} = \frac{28}{20} + \frac{15}{20} = \frac{43}{20}$$

How to automate this process, the algorithm that leads to the sum of any two fractions? The bad news is that it takes eight steps to reach the result. Some of these steps can be done mentally, but never skipped.

The most hardworking, and therefore most rewarding, is the application of the least common multiple (LCM), to obtain the equalization of the denominators. Yes, the common denominator will be the LCM of the denominators of the plots. Once this LCM was obtained, we proceeded to assemble the equivalent fractions, discovering the new numerators. The most practical method of obtaining the LCM is that of division by prime factors, which is the joint decomposition into prime factors. A prime number is the natural number that has exactly two distinct divisors, one being the number 1, which is a divisor of any number. The number 4, for example, is not prime, it is composed, because besides divisors 1 and 4 there is also the divisor 2.

To add, for example, 5/4 + 1/5, we have to find the LCM between 4 and 5. Let us pretend that we still don't know how much it is. We will divide the values successively by the prime factors 2, 3, 5, 7, 11, 13, 17, 19, and so on, as possible, and how many times it is necessary.

We do:

$$
\begin{array}{cc|c}
4,5 & & 2 \\
2,5 & & 2 \\
1,5 & & 5 \\
\hline
1,1 & & 20
\end{array}
$$

While multiplying the prime factors from top to bottom, we have 2*2*5 = 20.

The denominator of the fraction will therefore be changed to 20.

To find the new numerators, we just find the factor that brings the old denominator to this value of LCM. To do this, we simply divide the LCM 20 by the old denominators, one by one.

$$\frac{3}{4} + \frac{1}{5} = \frac{...}{20} + \frac{...}{20}$$

After dividing and finding this factor, we will multiply it by the corresponding numerator. The first factor we will multiply it by 3. The second factor, by 1. And we will fill in the blanks above.

$$\frac{3}{4} + \frac{1}{5} = \frac{15}{20} + \frac{4}{20} = \frac{19}{20}$$

What we did was: 20 divided by 4, which gave 5, and 5*3, which gave 15. After, 20 divided by 5, which gave 4, and 4*1, which gave 4.

The steps were: (1) setting up the account, 3/4 + 1/5; (2) arming the LCM key with the denominators; (3) dividing by prime factors; (4) multiplying the resulting factors to find the LCM, which is the new denominator; (5) arranging the new denominators in the fractions; (6) dividing each by the old denominator; (7) multiplying the result by the corresponding numerator, then writing it in its new position; (8) writing the sum of the new numerators over the common denominator, arriving at the result.

If instead of two fractions we add three or more, the path is the same. We make LCM with three or more denominators and add the resulting three or more fractions, now having equal denominators.

If instead of fractions with only a plus sign, we also have a minus sign, the path again is the same, just decrease when the sign "+" appears.

Exercise **P0.03**
Make the fractions additions below.

A) $\dfrac{2}{3} + \dfrac{3}{4} - \dfrac{1}{2}$

Resolution:

LCM:

3, 4, 2	2
3, 2, 1	2
3, 1, 1	3
1, 1, 1	12

$$\frac{2}{3} + \frac{3}{4} - \frac{1}{2} = \frac{8}{12} + \frac{9}{12} - \frac{6}{12} = \frac{11}{12}$$

B) 2/5 + 1/3 + 3/4. C) 1/4 + 1/6 + 3/2. D) 2/3 + 1/7 + +3/4. E) 2/7 + 1/2 - 3/5. F) 3/5 + 1/2 - 1/4.

Multiplying fractions is a much simpler operation than adding, because it involves much fewer steps than those eight.

To multiply two fractions, we just multiply their numerators, to obtain the new numerator, and their denominators, reaching the new denominator. The only "complicated" thing is that we must always be attentive to simplifications. Within multiplication, the numerator of a fraction can be simplified with the denominator of another, because multiplication is commutative. The most convenient is to simplify in the middle of the process, not leaving it to the end of the account.

To make (3/2)*(5/7) just do

$$\frac{3}{2} * \frac{5}{7} = \frac{15}{14}$$

Here we had no simplifications to make.
But let's do it now (3/4)*(8/5).
"Cutting" 8 with 4, we will have:

$$\frac{3}{4} * \frac{8}{5} = \frac{3}{1} * \frac{2}{5} = \frac{6}{5}$$

And how to divide one fraction by another? As we said before, division is multiplication by the inverse, that is, by the inverse fraction.

So (a/b):(c/d) = (a/b)*(d/c).
To perform (4/5) :(3/7), we do:

$$\frac{4}{5} : \frac{3}{7} = \frac{4}{5} * \frac{7}{3} = \frac{28}{15}$$

Important: since the priority of multiplication and division in arithmetic expressions is the same, the order in which these operations appear in the accounts is what matters.

So:

$$\frac{1}{3} : \frac{2}{5} * \frac{7}{3} = \frac{1}{3} * \frac{5}{2} * \frac{7}{3} = \frac{35}{18}$$

Exercise **P0.04**

Find out the result of the operations below.

A) $\frac{3}{4} * \frac{4}{5} : \frac{3}{10}$

Resolution:

$$\frac{3}{4} * \frac{4}{5} : \frac{3}{10} = \frac{3}{4} * \frac{4}{5} * \frac{10}{3} = \frac{1}{1} * \frac{1}{1} * \frac{2}{1} = \frac{2}{1} = 2$$

B) (3/2)*(1/4)*(3/7). C) (1/3)*(4/3):(5/3). D) (3/8)*(4/7):(5/3). E) (3/7)*(5/6)*(7/10). F) (1/4):(7/9).

We give the name of decimal fraction to the fraction whose denominator is a power of 10, that is, a number like 10, 100, 1000, 10000, and so on. The numbers 3/10, 157/100 and 21/1000 are decimal fractions.

Decimal fractions are easily transformed into decimal numerals, which are floating-point numerals. To do this, just count the number of zeros after 1, in the denominator. This amount will be the number of places after the dot. So, on 21/1000, we have three zeros. Since 21 has only two digits, we complete it with leading zeros: 21/1000 = 0.021.

The number 157/100 is written:

$$\frac{157}{100} = 1.57.$$

To return, from decimal to fractional form, just count the spaces after the dot: each will be a zero after the digit 1 of the denominator.

So:

$$0.13 = \frac{13}{100} \; ; \; 14.9 = \frac{149}{10} \; ; \; 0.007 = \frac{7}{1000} \; .$$

To add two numbers written with floating-point, it is not necessary, as in subtraction, to complete the spaces to the right with zeros to equal their quantity, but it is convenient to do so.

Adding 3.46 and 16.452 means doing: 3.460 + 16.452. To set up the account, we must write dot under dot. Our result will be 19,912.

To subtract, we must always match the number of places after the dot, then having a dot under a dot when setting up the account. So, 12.4 - 7.513 requires that we write 12.400 - 7.513. By borrowing 1, as we learned in the first school year, our operation results in 4,887.

When we are going to *multiply two numbers with dot*, we do not need to have a dot under a dot, as we do in addition and subtraction. What we have to do here is to count the number of places after the dot in both factors, this being the number of places after the dot in the result. This accounting is made only at the end of the operation, during which we ignore the role of dots.

So, to multiply 3.6 by 2.754 we have the factor 2.754 at the top and the factor 3.6 under it, since it is always convenient to put the one with the least number below. After multiplying, we reached number 99144, which is not yet the answer. One factor has a place after the dot and the other has three. The result must have four places (1 + 3) after the dot: 9.9144. When in work situations we do these operations on the calculator, we have to master this knowledge to be able to check the result on the display - otherwise we will be controlled by the machine: a blind person guiding another blind person.

For the *division of decimals*, the most convenient way is to eliminate the dot of the divisor, making the corresponding adjustment in the dividend.

Dividing 56.924 by 0.16 will first mean moving the 0.16 point two places to the right (this is the same as multiplying the value by 100), obtaining 16 integers. The same type of change has to be made in the dividend (which is a numerator). While passing the dot two places to the right, we get 5692.4. Now we do 5692.4:0.16. Our result will be 355,775.

The dot is placed in the quotient when the entire part of the dividend is exhausted. Without secrets.

If we are going to divide 140 by 2.9, we simply move one place to the right on the divisor, getting 29. The dividend has to change to 1400. The quotient will be 48.275862...

The priority in the resolution of numerical expressions obeys, as for the brackets, brackets and braces, exactly in this order: first brackets, "( )"; then square brackets, "[ ]"; and, finally, braces, "{ }". We must remember that parentheses mean "times". As for operations, the order is: first, powers and roots; second, multiplication and division; third, addition and subtraction.

Let us solve the expression below.

$$5^2\{1+2[5 + 18:(3 + 2{*}3)]\}$$

We have:

$$5^2\{1+2[5 + 18:(3 + 6)]\}$$
$$5^2\{1+2[5 + 18:9]\}$$
$$5^2\{1+2[5 + 2]\}$$
$$5^2\{1+2{*}7\}$$
$$5^2\{1+14\}$$
$$5^2{*}15$$
$$25{*}15 = 375.$$

Exercise **P0.05**
Solve the arithmetic expressions below.

A) 20:{-4 + 2[1 + 2(9 − 3*2)]} − 4.
Resolution:
20:{-4 + 2[1 + 2(9 − 3*2)]} − 4
20:{-4 + 2[1 + 2(9 − 6)]} − 4
20:{-4 + 2[1 + 2*3]} − 4
20:{-4 + 2[1 + 6]} − 4
20:{-4 + 2*7} − 4
20:{-4 + 14} − 4
20:10 − 4
2 − 4 = -2.
   B) {13 + 3[2+4(1+3*5)]} − 3². C) 2{4+ 2[5+2(16 − 4*2)]}.
D) {-1 +3[2(9 − 4*2)] − 2} + 7. E) {7 + 4[1 + 5(1 + 9:3)]} − 10:2.

How to add *algebraic fractions*? At first glance it seems difficult, but it is a mistake. Once the student gets used to the operation, it becomes simpler than that of purely numerical fractions.

Let us do the following operation (com a ≠ 0 e b ≠ 0):

$$\frac{4}{a} + \frac{5}{b}$$

We must first find the LCM between **a** and **b**, which are the denominators. It is simply the ab product. (To find LCM of expressions like ab, ac and abd, we will group all the factors in the product, without repeating those already included. The LCM will be abcd.)
Our sum will be:

$$\frac{4}{a} + \frac{5}{b} = \frac{...}{ab} + \frac{...}{ab}$$

The division of ab by **a** gives **b** (in ab/a, "cut" a with **a**), which multiplied by 4 results in 4b. In the second plot, ab by **b** gives **a**, which multiplied by 5 gives 5a. We will have:

$$\frac{4}{a} + \frac{5}{b} = \frac{4b}{ab} + \frac{5a}{ab} = \frac{4b+5a}{ab}$$

Exercise **P0.06**
Make the additions below.
A) a/c − 3c/(ab)
Resolution:
The LCM is abc.

$$\frac{a}{c} - \frac{3c}{ab} = \frac{a^2b}{abc} - \frac{3c^2}{abc} = \frac{a^2b-3c^2}{abc}$$

B) x/a − 2y/(ax). C) a/x + b/(xy). D) a/b + c/a. E) a²/c − b²/a.

Percentage

A ratio is an operation between two values, the antecedent and the consequent, understood as a relationship established by the preposition "in" between them, and a percentage is a ratio whose consequent is worth 100. A ratio expressed as a fraction has as its antecedent the numerator, and as its consequent, the denominator, obviously.

If, from the work meetings that my study group held, I attended 5 out of 8, what is the ratio for my attendance?

If I participated in 5 of 8, the ratio is 5 to 8, or 5 octaves, which can be represented by the fraction 5/8.

What was the percentage of my attendance, that is, if the antecedent is 100, if there are 100 meetings, what will be the antecedent?

The calculation is done through a "rule of three", a proportion in which we match two ratios, with antecedent and consequent, to find one of the values, the other three being given.

In this case we have x/100 = 5/8.

We can solve the rule of three as we learned in the elementary course, but that means that we will always have the value 100 multiplied by the antecedent (numerator) of the second ratio (fraction), with a result that will be divided by the consequent (denominator of the fraction). The value we find for **x**, when placed above the denominator 100, will represent the percentage, and can be written as x%, that is, **x** per 100, or x/100.

In practice, we take the division of 5 by 8, numerator by denominator, and multiply the result by 100, that is, we make the dot jump two decimal places (or orders) to the right.

Making

5 |8̲, we get 0.625. So our value **y**, which is the value x%, will be y = 62.5%.

Answering "how much percent gives" is the same as answering "how many hundredths gives". Thus, saying 47% is the same as saying 47/100, or 0.47.

Exercise **P0.07**

Write as a percentage the ratio given below.

A) 7 in 16.

Resolution: y = 7:16 = 0,4375 = 43,75%

B) 3 in 4. C) 3 in 10. D) 3 in 8. E) 9 in 40.

Exercise **P0.08**

Write as a percentage the ratio represented in the painted part of the figure.

A) |■|□|□|□|□|□|□|□|

Resolution: 1 |8̲ gives 0.125. So y = 1/8 = 0.125 = 1.25%

B) |■|■|■|□|□|□|□|□|

C) |■|■|■|■|□|□|□|□|

D) |■|■|■|□|□|

E) |■|■|■|■|■|□|□|□|

Rounding

In the percentages, we will adopt here the rounding to the hundredth place, whenever we do not have integer values, but values with dots. If the division is accurate to the tenth place, we will obviously not need to write 0 for the hundredth. So, instead of 4.80%, we will write 4.8%.

But how do we write y = 0.51392 as a percentage?

It will be rounded up to y = 51.39%.

And in the number y = 0.25835? Here we will make y = 25.84%

That final 2 of 0.51392 was waived, but the value 5 of 0.25835 was used (to change the previous place). Because?

The universal rounding rule is that in the first half of the final figures (0, 1, 2, 3, and 4) we dispense them (rounding down), but in the second half (5, 6, 7, 8, and 9) , we add 1 to the place that is preceding the digit, which will no longer be written.

Exercise P0.09
Round the values below to the tenth place.
A) 4:15
Resolution: 4 ⌊15 gives 0,2666... So y = 4/15 ≈ 0,3.
B) 12:7 C) 5:6 D) 200:3 E) 1,45555... (here, we just round)

Exercise **P0.10**
Round the values given below to integer number.
A) 15:2
Resolution: 15 ⌊2 gives 7,5. So y = 15/2 ≈ 7.
B) 1:6 C) 43:6 D) 28,71 E) 20:7

Exercise **P0.11**
Round to the nearest tenth of a thousandth each value given.

A) 90:7
Resolution: 90 $\lfloor$7 gives 12.857142... So y = 90/7 ≈ 12.8571.
B) 25:3 C) 8:9 D) 50:7 E) 30.243567

Exercise **P0.12**
Write as a percentage each result of the previous exercise.
Resolution: A) y = 90/7 ≈ 12.8571 = 1285.71%.

Exercise **P0.13**
Anthony had an amount and, of that total, he provided part of it as a loan. Say how much percent this part represents if he borrowed:
A) $40 in $210
Resolution: 40 $\lfloor$210 gives 0.190476... So y = 40/210 ≈ ≈ 0.1905 = 19.05%.
B) $20 in $90. C) $10 in $110. D) $800 in $1400. E) $120 in $1500.

Percent

Percent is the fraction of some quantity obtained through percentage.
For example, we have 200 grams of a product and we will take 15%. How many grams will it give? The value 10% is the percentage, whereas what we get in grams will be the percent. To reach the result just multiply 15% by the total. As 15% is the representation of the fraction 15/100, and the fraction "of" a number is the product of it by that number, so the percentage **u** will be given by u = 15%*200 = (15/100)*200 = (15)*2 = 30. The result is u = 30 grams. (In the operation, we cut, i. e., we simplify, the two zeros of 200 with the two zeros of the denominator 100.)

Exercise **Po.14**

Obtain the percent **u** referring to the percentage of the total given.

A) 18% of 70 m

Resolution:

$$U = \frac{18}{100} \, {*}70 = \frac{18}{10} \, {*} \frac{7}{1} = \frac{126}{10} = 12.6. \text{ Ans.: } u = 12.6 \text{ m.}$$

Another way: 0.18*70 =...

B) 5% of \$300. C) 140% of 30 kg. D) 200% of 45 cm. E) 20% of 88 km.

Price increase

If we have a commodity with a given price and we want to apply an increase on it, by a certain percentage, what we learn in the elementary course is to multiply this rate of increase by the price and, once the value has been found, add it to the original price given.

Thus, if the original price was **p** and the increase index was **a**, to obtain the new price **n**, we do:

$$p + a{*}p = n.$$

Now, after the elementary course, we highlight the price p. We will have:

$$n = p(1 + a), \text{ or } n = p(100\% + a).$$

We already know that the 1/1 ratio is the same as the 100% percentage, which is worth 100/100.

The same idea of the formula above applies to a discount on the price **p**, since the discount is an index with a negative sign.

Given a price **p**, a new value **v** after an index discount **a** will be:

$$v = p(1 - a), \text{ or } v = p(100 - a).$$

Exercise **Po.15**

Determine the new price **n** after one applies to a price **p** an increase of:

A) 13%, in p = $420

Resolution:

n = 420(100%+13%) = 420*113% = 420*113/100 = 42*113/10 = 4746/10 = 474.60.

B) 110%, in p = $80. C) 15%, in p = $50. D) 20%, in p = $240 . E) 1%, in p = $300

Exercise **Po.16**

Determine the new price **v** after one applies to a price **p** the discount of:

A) 14%, in p = $382

Resolution:

A = 382(100% - 14%) = 382*86% = 382*86/100 = 32852/100 = 328.52.

B) 8%, in p = $90. C) 18%, in p = 400. D) 20%, in p = 490. E) 17%, in p = $88.

Exercise **Po.17**

Given the new price **n** and the old price **p**, determine the percentage of increase.

A) n = $800, p = $500.

Resolution: 500(100%+x)=800 ⇔ 500(1+x)=800 ⇔ 1+x=800/500 ⇔ 1+x=8/5 ⇔ 1+x=1.6 ⇔ x=1.6-1.0 ⇔ x=0.6 ⇔ x=0.6*100% ⇔ x=60%.

B) n = $500, p = $160. C) n = $180, p = $120. D) n = $145, p = $20. E) n = $90, p = $60.

Exercise **Po.18**

Given the discounted price **v** and the old price **p**, determine the discount percentage.

A) v = $350, p = $500.

Resolution: 500(100%-x)=350 ⇔ 500(1-x)=350 ⇔

$\Leftrightarrow$ 1-x=350/500 $\Leftrightarrow$ 1-x=35/50 $\Leftrightarrow$ 1-x=0.7 $\Leftrightarrow$ -x=0.7-1.0 $\Leftrightarrow$
$\Leftrightarrow$ -x=-0.3 $\Leftrightarrow$ x=0.3 $\Leftrightarrow$ x=0.3*100% $\Leftrightarrow$ x=30%.

B) v = $160, p = $800.   C) v = $220, p = $400. D) v = $270, p = $340. E) v = $60, p = $70

Exercise P0.19

A segment has length **n** when dilated, and length **p**, before dilation. Calculate the percentage of dilation it has undergone.

A) n = 600 cm, p = 560 cm.

$$\underline{\hspace{6cm}}\ p$$
$$\underline{\hspace{6cm}}\ n$$

Resolution: 560(100%+x)=600 $\Leftrightarrow$ 560(1+x)=600 $\Leftrightarrow$
$\Leftrightarrow$ 1+x=600/560 $\Leftrightarrow$ 1+x=60/56 $\Leftrightarrow$ 1+x=1.0714285... $\Leftrightarrow$
$\Leftrightarrow$ x $\approx$ 1.0714 - 1.0 $\Leftrightarrow$ x = 0.0714 $\Leftrightarrow$ x = 7.14%.

B) n = 40 cm, p = 38 cm. C) n = 500 cm, p = 400 cm. D) n = 80 cm, p = 64 cm. A) n = 8 cm, p = 3 cm.

Exercise P0.20

A merchant has sold for a value **n** a commodity that he had bought for price **p**. Calculate the percentage of profit in the transaction.

A) n = $500, p = $410.

Resolution: 410(100%+x)=500 $\Leftrightarrow$ 410(1+x)=500 $\Leftrightarrow$
$\Leftrightarrow$ 1+x=500/410 $\Leftrightarrow$ 1+x=50/41 $\Leftrightarrow$ 1+x=1.21951... $\Leftrightarrow$ x $\approx$
$\approx$ 1.2195-1.0 $\Leftrightarrow$ x=0.2195 $\Leftrightarrow$ x=21.95%.

B) n = $460, p = $400. C) n = $1220, p = $800. D) n = $400, p = $350. E) n = $90, p = $80.

Arithmetic progression

A number *sequence* is an ordered set $(a_1, a_2, a_3,...)$ that can be finite, for example, (2, 8, 3, 8, 0, 7), or infinite, such as (1/2 , 1/4, 1/8, 1/16, ...). It is usually defined as a function f: A $\rightarrow$ R,

$A \subset N - \{0\}$, with image set $(a_1, a_2, a_3, a_4,...)$.

The values, or the images, of a sequence can be given by a *formation law*, usually a formula, or they can be defined individually, as in the first example above. To see how this works, let us calculate the first four elements of the infinite sequence given by the formation law $a_n = 3n^2 - 4$.

The number **n**, of the function's starting set, runs, by default, the set of positive integers: 1, 2, 3, 4, 5, ... These numbers are the indexes of the images a_1, a_2, a_3,...

So, we do (starting with $n = 1$):

$a_n = 3n^2 - 4$

$a_1 = 3(1)^2 - 4 = 3{*}1 - 4 = 3 - 3 = -1,$

$a_2 = 3(2)^2 - 4 = 3{*}3 - 4 = 9 - 4 = 5,$

$a_3 = 3(3)^2 - 4 = 3{*}9 - 4 = 27 - 4 = 23,$

$a_4 = 3(4)^2 - 4 = 3{*}16 - 4 = 48 - 4 = 44.$

Our sequence will be: $(-1, 5, 23, 44, ...)$.

A very special type of sequence that arises from a formation law is the *arithmetic progression* (AP). It is defined as the sequence, or progression, in which each term, starting from the first, a_1, is equal to the previous term plus a fixed value, called *step*, which is also a rate. Thus, a PA whose first term is $a_1 = 5$ and whose step is $r = -2$ is given by $(5, 3, 1, -1, -3, ...)$. Another, which has first term $a_1 = 4$ and ratio $r = 3$, is explained as $(4, 7, 10, 13, ...)$.

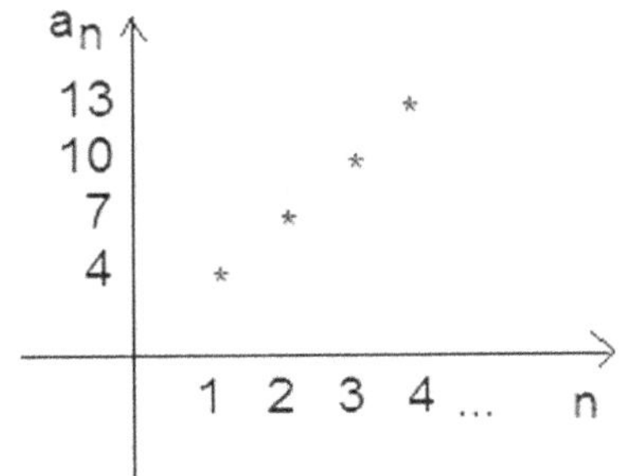

(Graphic of a increasing AP)

An arithmetic progression can be *decreasing* (has a negative step), *increasing* (has a positive step) or *constant* (has a zero step).

Exercise **P0.21**
Find the reason (or step) for the given arithmetic progression.

A) $(2, 6, 10, 14, ...)$
Resolution (we subtract the previous term from any term):
$r = 6-2 = 4$.

B) $(-3, -1, 1, 3, 5, ...)$. C) $(10, 15, 20, 25, ...)$. D) $(1/2, 3/2, 5/2, 7/2, ...)$. E) $(4, 3, 2, 1 ...)$.

There is a formula that provides the general term (a_n) for any arithmetic progression, starting from its first term and its reason. We see that to obtain the second term we add the first, a_1, with the step **r**. From there, to get to the third term, we add the rate **r** again, that is, from the first term, we add the step twice, $2r$. To reach the fourth term, we add the step again, leaving $3r$. We had: $a_1 = a_1+0$, $a_2 = a_1+1r$, $a_3 = a1 + 2r$, $a_4 = = a_1+3r$. This index **n** appears in the second member of the equality as its predecessor, by multiplying **r**. Thus, our formula for the general term is:

$$a_n = a_1 + (n-1)r.$$

Exercise **P0.22**
Find the twentieth term for each given arithmetic progression.

A) $a_1 = 7$, $r = 3$.
Resolution:
$a_n = a_1 + (n-1)r$
$a_{20} = 7 + (20-1)*3 = 7 +19*3 = 7 + 57 = 64$.

B) $a_1 = 1$, $r = 5$. C) $a_1 = -9$, $r = 2$. D) $a_1 = 50$, $r = -6$. E) $a_1 = 5/2$, $r = 3/2$.

Exercise **Po.23**

Find the step and the sixteenth term of the arithmetic progression.

A) $a_1 = 3$, $a_7 = 33$.

Resolution:

$a_n = a_1 + (n-1)r$ $a_n = a_1 + (n-1)r$

$33 = 3 + (7-1)*r$ $a_{16} = 3 + (16-1)*5$

$33 = 3 + 6r$ $a_{16} = 3 + 15*5$

$33 - 3 = 6r$ $a_{16} = 3 + 75$

$6r = 30 \Leftrightarrow r = 30/6 = 5$. $a_{16} = 78$.

B) $a_1 = 2$, $a_4 = 14$.   C) $a_1 = -3$, $a_6 = 32$.   D) $a_1 = 5$, $a_9 = 21$. E) $a_1 = 3$, $a_8 = 45$.

Exercise **Po.24**

Using the medium term property of AP [$a_2 = (a_1 + a_3)/2$, or, more generally, $a_k = (a_{k-p} + a_{k+p})/2$, k, p $\in$ Z_+ - {0}]], or characteristic property, according to which each term is the arithmetic mean of two equidistant terms, obtain the value of **x**.

A) (4, 2x+3, 18).

Resolution:

$$a_2 = \frac{a_1 + a_3}{2}$$

$$2x+3 = \frac{4+18}{2}$$

$$2x+3 = 22/2$$

$$2x = 11$$

$$x = \frac{11}{2}$$

B) (3, 2x+6, 17).   C) (-1, x+4, 15).   D) (20, 3x-3, 4).   E) (7, 2x+9, 22).

Exercise **Po.25**

While knowing that the sum of the first terms of the AP is the average of the extremes multiplied by the number of terms, $S_n = (a_1 + a_n)n/2$, obtain the sum of the first n terms of each arithmetic progression below, given a_1 and **r**.

A) $a_1 = 5$, $r = 3$, $n = 18$.

Resolution:

$a_n = a_1 + (n-1)r$

$a_{18} = 5 + (18-1)*3 = 5 + 17*3 = 5 + 51 = 56.$

$$S_n = \frac{(a_1 + a_n)n}{2}$$

$S_{18} = (5 + 56)*18/2 = 61*18/2 = 61*9 = 549.$

B) $a_1 = 3$, $r = 2$, $n = 41$. C) $a_1 = 10$, $r = 4$, $n = 20$. D) $a_1 = 6$, $r = 7$, $n = 16$. E) $a_1 = 45$, $r = -3$, $n = 23$.

Geometric progression

Another special type of sequence, very similar to AP, is the *geometric progression* (GP). It is defined as the sequence, or progression, in which each term, starting from the first, a_1, is equal to the previous term multiplied by a fixed value, called ratio.

A PG whose first term is $a_1 = 3$ and whose ratio is $q = 2$ is given by (3, 6, 12, 24, 48, ...). Other examples are (16, 8, 4, 2, ...), with ratio $q = 1/2$; (5, 5, 5, 5, ...), with ratio $q = 1$; (1, -2, 4, -6, 16, ...), with reason $q = -2$ (q: quotient).

A geometric progression can be increasing (has a ratio greater than 1), decreasing (has a positive ratio less than 1), oscillating (has a negative ratio) or constant (has a ratio equal to 1).

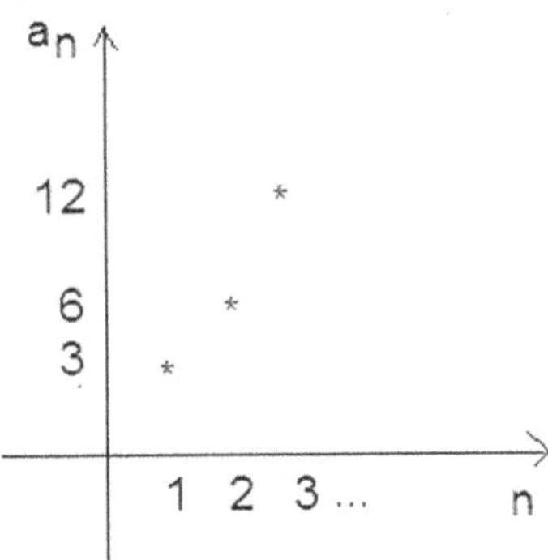

(Graphic of an increasing GP)

Since the following terms are obtained by multiplying the ratio, in order to arrive at the formula for the general term of the PG we have to successively multiply the ratio **q**, after the first term a_1. Thus, the formula will be given by:

$$a_n = a_1 q^{n-1}$$

The characteristic property of GP is related to the geometric mean. Each GP term is equal to the geometric mean of two equidistant terms. Thus, the first term is the geometric mean between the first and the third terms, for example.

$$a_2 = \sqrt{(a_1 {}^* a_3)}.$$

In the finite GP of positive terms (2, x, 50), the value of **x**, second term, must be 10. Let us check: $a_2 = \sqrt{(a_1 {}^* a_3)}$, then $x = +\sqrt{(2 {}^* 50)} = +\sqrt{100} = 10$. Without the information that the terms are positive, we would have to take into account both the positive and the negative response. We would have $a_2 = \pm\sqrt{(a_1 {}^* a_{13})}$. Note that if we have the PG (-2, x, -50), the value of **x** is necessarily positive. Why does this happen?

More generally, we have:

$$a_k = \sqrt{(a_{k-p} * a_{k+p})}, \; k, p \in Z_+ - \{0\}.$$

The geometric mean, also called the harmonic mean in Plane Geometry, is represented as a segment within the circle that has length **h** given by the square root of the product of two sections, of measures **a** and **b**, that complete the diameter. The sequence (a, h, b) obviously forms a GP.

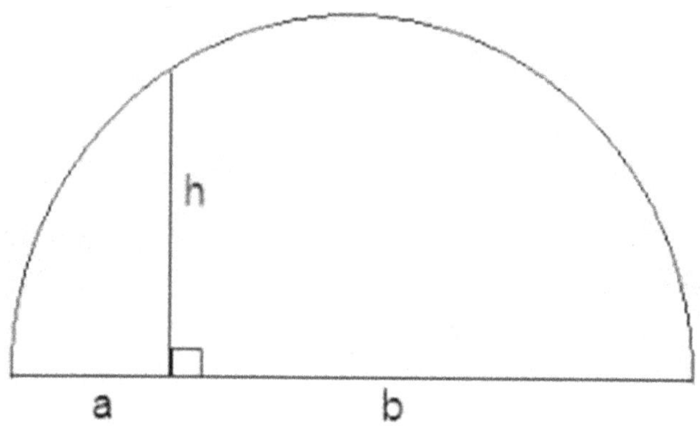

(Geometric or harmonic mean)

The formula for the sum of the first **n** terms of the GP has a demonstration that demands a little more work. The most usual presentation of it is given by:

$$S_n = \frac{a_1\left(1-q^n\right)}{1-q}$$

How much does the sum of the first 10 terms of the GG give with $a_1 = 3$ and $q = 2$? Just do:

$$S_n = \frac{a_1(1-q^n)}{1-q}$$

$$S_n = \frac{3(1-2^{10})}{1-2} = \frac{3(1-1024)}{-1} = \frac{3(-1023)}{-1} =$$

$$= \frac{-3(1023)}{-1} = 3069.$$

The demonstration of the formula is simple and knowing it can help with memorization.

First, we write the sum with the explicit values:

$S_n = a_1+a_2+a_3+...+a_n.$

Writing so that the reason q appears, we have:

$S_n = a_1+a_1q+a_1q^2+a_1q^3+...+a_1q^{n-1}$

A little trick now is to multiply the terms of this equality by the ratio **q**:

$qS_n = a_1q+a_1q^2+a_1q^3+a_1q^4+...+a_1q^n.$

Finally, we subtract this last equality from the previous one.

$S_n = a_1+a_1q+a_1q^2+a_1q^3+...+a_1q^{n-1}$

$(-1) \quad qS_n = a_1q+a_1q^2+a_1q^3+a_1q^4+...+a_1q^n.$

$S_n-qS_n = a_1-a_1q^n.$

We will have $S_n-qS_n = a_1-a_1q^n \Leftrightarrow S_n(1-q) = a_1(1-q^n)$. Passing the factor 1-q to the second member, we come to the end:

$$S_n = \frac{a_1(1-q^n)}{1-q}$$

As we wanted to demonstrate
(Qed: *Quod erat demonstrandum*).

Unlike the case of AP, it makes sense to calculate the sum of the infinite terms of a GP, since the ratio **q** has a modulus less than 1. In this case, we say that the GP is a *convergent series*, as it converges to a number. If **q** has a modulus less than 1, $|q|<1$, that power q^n in the formula of the sum of the first **n** terms will tend to zero as **n** goes to infinity. If, for example, $q = 1/2$, when we raise it to 1, 2, 3, 4, etc., we see that the values are falling, and are approaching zero: 1/2, 1/4, 1/8 , 1/16,...

For infinite terms, therefore, we can forget the index **n**, making $S = a_1(1-0)/(1-q)$.

So, the formula for the sum of PG for infinite terms is given by:

$$S = \frac{a_1}{1-q} \text{ , whenever } |q|<1.$$

If we want to know how much the sum of GP (5, 5/2, 5/4, 5/8, ...) is worth, that is, of GP with $a_1 = 5$ and $q = 1/2$, we will do:

$$S = \frac{a_1}{1-q}$$

$$S = \frac{5}{1-1/2} = \frac{5}{1/2} = 5*\frac{2}{1} = 5*2 = 10.$$

Exercise **Po.26**
Find out the ratio for each given geometric progression.
A) (3, 12, 48, 192,...).
Resolution: $q = 12/3 = 4$.
B) (2, 6, 18, 54,...). C) (1, 1/2, 1/4, 1/8,...). D) ((4, -4, 4, -4, 4,...). E) (3, 9, 27, 81,...).

Exercise **Po.27**
Using the general term formula, obtain the twelfth term for each GP.
A) $a_1 = 7$, $q = 2$.
Resolution:
$a_n = a_1 q^{n-1}$
$a_{12} = 7*2^{12-1} = 7*2^{11} = 7*2048 = 14336.$

B) $a_1 = 5$, $q = -2$. C) $a_1 = 3$, $q = \frac{1}{2}$. D) $a_1 = 4$, $q = 3$. E) $a_1 = 1$, $q = 2$.

Exercise **Po.28**
Interpolate, or insert, **k** positive geometric means (intermediate terms) between the given values.
A) 2 e 81/8, k = 3.
Resolution:
As we are going to insert three terms between 2 and 81/8, forming a GP, then we have five terms (three inserted plus the two extremes). Thus, $a_1 = 2$ and $a_5 = 81/8$.

$a_n = a_1 q^{n-1}$
$81/8 = 2 * q^{5-1}$
$81/16 = q^4$
$q^4 = 81/16 \Rightarrow q = + \sqrt[4]{(81/16)} \Rightarrow + \sqrt[4]{(3/2)^4} = +3/2$.

The GP will be: (2, 3, 9/2, 27/4, 81/8). (It was just multiplying 2 by 3/2 and so on.)
Inserted terms: 3, 9/2, 27/4.
B) 1/2 e 125/16, k = 2. C) 2 e 250, k = 2. D) 1 e 1/81, k = 3. E) 3 e 3/16, k = 3.

Exercise **Po.29**
Using the medium term property of the GP, find the value of **x** in the given GP, of positive terms.
A) (5, x+8, 45).
Resolution:
$a_2 = \pm\sqrt{(a_1 * a_3)}$.
$x+8 = +\sqrt{(5 * 45)}$
$x+8 = +\sqrt{225}$
$x+8 = 15 \Leftrightarrow x = 15 - 8 \Leftrightarrow x = 7$.
B) (3, 2x+6, 48). C) (1, 2x+3, 49). D) (2, 3x+6, 162). E) (4, x+5, 16).

Exercise **Po.30**
Obtain the sum of the first eight terms of the given GP.
A) (2, 6, 18,...).

Resolution:

$q = 6/2 = 3$.

$S_n = a_1(1-q^n)/(1-q)$

$S_n = 2(1 - 3^8)/(1-3) = 2(1-6541)/(-2) = -2(6540)/(-2) = 3270$.

B) (3, 6, 12,...). C) (1, 4, 16,...). D) (2, 4, 8,...). E) (1/2, 3/2, 9/2,...).

Exercise **Po.31**

Obtain the sum of all the terms of the GP, given the first term and the ratio.

A) $a_1 = 9$, $q = ¼$.

Resolution:

$S = a_1/(1-q)$

$S = 9/(1-1/4) = 9/[(4-1)/4] = 9/(3/4) = 9*4/3 = 3*4 = 12$.

B) $a_1 = -7$, $q = 1/6$. C) a1 $= 5$, $q = 1/3$. D) $a_1 = 2$, $q = 1/5$. E) $a_1 = 5$, $q = ¾$.

Supplementary exercises

So.01

Make:

$- 6 + (-3)*(+5) - (-18):(+2) + 5*(-4)$.

So.02

Make the following additions of fractions:

a) $3/5 + 1/2 - 4/7$

b) $1/5 + 2/3 + 1/3 + 2/9$

So.03

Make:

a) $(3/8)*(2/7)*(4/5)$

b) $(1/3)*(6/5)*(2/3):(3/4)$

So.04

Solve the arithmetic expression below.

$5*\{-1 + 3[2 - 4(11 - 4*3)]\} - 3(7 - 4)$.

S0.05
Carry out, knowing that a ≠ 0 and b ≠ 0:
a) 5/a – 2a/3b
b) 7b/2a + a/5b

S0.06
Write as a percentage:
a) 12 in 20
b) 13 in 8
c) 15/16

S0.07
Round to the hundredth place:
a) 7/15   b) 12/13 c) 0,0289   d) 15/32

S0.08
Write as a percentage the result of the operations below.
a) 20:3 b) 5:9   c) 17:7   d) 11:32

S0.09
Lucius had $300 in his pocket, but he lent his friend Manuel $40. When percent did this loan represent in relation to what Lucius had?

S0.10
Determine the percent for the indicated percentage:
a) 15% of $500   b) 10% of 80 m   c) 7,5% of 900 kg

S0.11
Give the new price **n** after applying the indicated percentage increase over the given price.
a) 14% in p = $200   b) 105% in p = $70   c) 45% in p = = $250

So.12

Give the new price **v** after applying the indicated discount to the price **p**.

a) 12% in p = \$400   b) 17,5% in p = \$800   c) 9% in p = = \$320

So.13

Obtain the percentage increase given the new price **n** and the old price **p**.

a) n = \$80, p = \$50. b) n = \$100, p = \$75. c) n = \$400, p = \$300.

So.14

Determine the percentage increase by knowing the discounted price **v** and the old price **p**.

a) v = \$200, p = \$400. b) v = \$70, p = \$86. c) v = \$400, p = \$750.

So.15

Flavius bought merchandise for \$480 and sold it a week later for \$540. What percentage of profit did he earn?

So.16

Give the step, or rate, of the arithmetic progression (AP).
a) (1, 5, 9, 13,...) b) (10, 8, 6, 4,...) c) (2, 2, 2, 2,...)

So.17

Find the twenty-third term of the AP of rate r = 4 and the first term a_1 = -8.

So.18

By the property of the medium term of the AP, find the value of **x** in the AP of three terms.

a) (5, 4x+4, 11)   b) (-2, 7x-11, 8)

S0.19

Obtain the sum of the first 40 terms of the AP (-12, -5, 2, ...).

S0.20

Determine the ratio for the given geometric progression (GP).

a) (5, 10, 20, 40,...)   b) (3, -3, 3, -3,...)   c) (16, 4, 1,...)

S0.21

Using the general term formula, find the eleventh term of the GP (1/2, 1, 2, ...).

S0.22

Using the mean term property of the GP, calculate the value of x in the GP for positive terms (3, 2x + 2, 48).

S0.23

Determine the sum of the first nine terms of the GP (4, 8, 16, ...).

S0.24

Obtain the sum of all the terms of the GG (6, 2, 2/3, ...).

Chapter 1 – Interest

When we lend a certain amount of capital C to someone or some institution, the remuneration we receive for our act is known as *interest*, which is calculated over a contracted period, day, month, year, etc. If the loan is extended beyond the unit of the established period, our remuneration becomes the "amount of interest".

Simple interest

Simple interest is the one that is calculated only on the basis of the capital initially invested, regardless of the number of periods of the loan or application.

It is not used in the market, except as a component of the duplicate discount formula (bank discount), which we will study later, or in rare cases among individuals, in short-term loans.

Its theoretical study, however, is very important, since from simple interest it becomes easy to understand the operation of other forms of remuneration of capital.

Exercise **P1.01**
Given an object (a road) of original measure **h**, for two consecutive days employees have to add a portion (stretch) equivalent to 5% of that value **h**. Calculate the value **j** of the addition and then the new measure M of the object.
A) h = 400 m, d = 3 days.

_______________________________ __ __ __

Resolution: j = h*(5/100)*d = 400*(5/100)*3 = 4*(5)*3 = = 60; m = h+j = 400+60 = 460. Answer: M = 460 m.
B) h = 500 kg, d = 2 days. C) 80 m², d = 3 days. D) 90 cm, d = 1 day. E) h = $700, d = 4 days.

Amount

The simple interest formula is given by
$$j = C*i*t,$$
where **t** is the time or period, **i** (*iuri*, interest in Latin; if it is 2%, for example, write 2/100, or 0.02) is the interest rate, C is the capital and **j** is the accumulated interest, not counting the invested capital.

The amount, however, includes the original capital. Its formula is given by

$$A = C+j.$$

Exercise **P1.02**
A benefactor lent $1,200 to a needy person, at simple monthly interest, of value **i**, over a period of **t** months. Calculate the interest at that stage.

A) i = 4%, t = 3 months.

Resolution: j = C*i*t = 1200*(4/100)*3 = 12*4*3 = 144. Answer: j = $144.

B) i = 2%, t = 4 months. C) i = 1%, t = 6 months. D) i = 3%, t = 5 months. E) i = 2.5%, t = 4 months.

Exercise **P1.03**
Calculate the amount for each situation in the previous exercise.

A) j = $144

Resolution: A = C+j = 1200+144 = 1344. Answer: A = = $1344.

Exercise **P1.04**
If a capital C has been lent for a certain time, calculate the interest for the amount A obtained.

A) A = $700, C=$450.

Resolution: A = C+j ⇔ 700 = 450+j ⇔ -j = 450-700 ⇔ -j = = -250 ⇔ j = 250. Answer: j = $250.

B) A = $1300, C=$1150. C) A = $1000, C=$800. D) A = = $3000, C=$2210. E) A = $8200, C=$540.

Installment

It is very common, when someone borrows at simple interest, to write off the debt by paying equal installments of the initial amount. For example, the citizen takes $600 for six months and goes down $600/6 monthly. So, when one returns $100 each month, along with interest payments, at the end of the term one owes nothing to the creditor.

Without taking into account interest, the original capital decreases in the hand of the debtor according to the following sequence:

Value: 600 500 400 300 200 100 0
Month: 0   1   2   3   4   5   6

As the debt decays forming a decreasing arithmetic progression, the interest debt will have the same character. Suppose the contract in the example above foresaw interest of 2% per month. So at the end of the first month, the rate is applied over $600, at the end of the second month, over $500, and so on (in each subperiod, t = 1).

We will have: $J_1 = 600*(2/100)*1 = 12$, $J_2 = 500*(2/100)*1 = 10$, $J_3 = 400*(2/100)*1 = 8$,... $J_6 = 100*(2/100)*1 = 2$.

Our sequence of interest paid is therefore 12, 10, 8, 6, 4, 2.

As there are few numbers, we can add them directly, but in a larger number of values we have to apply the formula of the sum of the arithmetic progression, created by Gauss as a child, $S_n = (1/2)*(a_1+a_n)*n$, which is the average of all the numbers multiplied by the quantity n.

In our example we will have:

$S_n = (1/2)*(12 + 2)*6 = (1/2)*14*6 = 7*6 = 42.$

Note that, if there was no rebate, the debtor would pay that amount 12 at the end of the first month until the end, which would result in $J = 600*0.02*6 = 72$. The amount here would be \$600+\$72, while in the previous situation it was \$600+\$42.

Whenever the debtor splits the debt over **n** periods as in the example, the interest rate payments **i** per period will be (remembering that t = 1):

$$J1 = C*i,$$
$$j2 = (C - C/n)*i = C*i*(1 - 1/n),$$
$$J3 = (C - 2c/n)*i = C*i*(1 - 2/n),$$

...

$$Jn\text{-}1 = [C - (n\text{-}2)*P/n]\,i = C*i*[1 - (n\text{-}2)/n],$$
$$Jn = [C - (n\text{-}1)*P/n]*i = C*i*[1 - (n\text{-}1)/n].$$

To find the total interest, J, we have to add the arithmetic progression J1+J2+... +Jn, which has first term $C*i$ and last term $C*i*[1 - (n\text{-}1)/n]$.

We will have:

$J = (1/2)\{C*i+C*i*[1\text{-}(n\text{-}1)/n]\}*n \Leftrightarrow J =$
$= (n/2)*C*i*[1+1 - (n\text{-}1)/n] \Leftrightarrow J =(n/2)*C*i*[(2*n-n+1)/n] \Leftrightarrow$
$\Leftrightarrow J = C*[(n+1)/2]*i,$ or $J = Ci(n+1)/2.$

The simple interest formula with installments will therefore be:

$$J = \frac{Ci(n+1)}{2}$$

Exercise **P1.05**

A customer borrows capital C, at simple interest of 3% per month, paying in installments for **n** months. Determine the interest and the amount M, in the cases below.

A) C = \$2400, n = 12 months.
Resolution:
$J = C*i*(n+1)/2$

J $=$ 2400*(3/100)*(12+1)/2 $=$ 24*3*(13/2) $=$ 12*3*13 $=$
$=$ 468. A = 2400+468 = 2868.

Answer: J = \$468, A = \$2868.

B) C = \$1000, n = 14 months. C) C = \$2100, n = 9 months.
D) C = \$10.000, n = 18 months. E) C = \$800, n = 11 months.

Discount of duplicate

To calculate the amount of the duplicates discount, or bank discount, the bank uses the idea of simple interest. It is a convenience of the bank first for paying in simple interest and not compound interest, which could result in a higher value, and second, due to the ease of calculations, since this type of operation is always urgent.

The fact occurs when the merchant, or other type of entrepreneur, has duplicate trades to receive within a period that for his needs is great. For example, a certain duplicate will mature on the 30th of the month, but the creditor needs that money on the 15th. He then goes to the bank, which buys the debt, that is, keeps the duplicate. That is when the discount comes in, because the bank is anticipating money. If the face value is \$8000, for example, the bank can offer \$7600 for the document. The entrepreneur will assess whether it is worth doing the transaction, and it almost always does, otherwise he does not need much the capital anticipation.

The formula for the current value, after discounting, is given by:

$$V = n - \frac{nip}{30}$$

Here, **n** is the nominal value, or face value, **i** is the interest rate and **p** the term, number of days, of the anticipation. The denominator 30 appears there because the business month is defined as having 30 days. In the final part of the formula, which gives the total discount, the value **n** corresponds to C and the value p/30 corresponds to **t**, of the simple interest formula. There is also the custom of presenting the formula with the value **n** in evidence: V = n (1 - i*p/30). The previous formula, however, is easier to use.

Exercise **P1.06**
A merchant intends to discount a duplicate with face value **n**, anticipated by **p** days, at a bank that charges interest rate **i**. Calculate the current value of the title for the possibilities below.

A) n = $4000, i=5%, p=45 days.

Resolution:

V = n – n*i*p/30 = 4000 – (4000*0.05*45/30) =
= 4000 – (40*5*1.5) = 4000 – 300 = 3700.

Answer: V = $3,700.00

B) $2000, i=4%, p=15 days. C) $9000, i=2.5%, p=60 days. D) $800, i=3%, p=40 days. E) $1600, i=2%, p=30 days.

Exercise **P1.07**
A businessman went to the bank to cash a duplicate of face value $5000, with interest rate i = 3%. Determine the term **p** of the discount, given the current value V of the security.

A) V = $4900.

Resolution:

V = n – n*i*p/30

4900 = 5000 – [5000*(3/100)*p/30]

4900 = 5000 – (50*3*p/30)

50*3*p/30 = 5000 – 4900

50*p/10 = 100

50*p = 100*10

50*p = 1000

p = 1000/50

p = 20. Answer: p = 20 days.

B) V = $4000 C) V = $4800 D) V = $3600 E) V = $4500

Compound interest

Compound interest is a type of income that at each capitalization period focuses on the accumulated amount, and not just on the original capital. This means that, if the rate period is the month, then after each month the capital to be remunerated involves the previous amount plus the interest for that month. Thus, if after three months the amount is A, in the fourth month the borrower's debt is A + j, with **j** calculated on the A of the third month.

Exercise **P1.08**

A man was hired in a company to increase a product (segment) of initial size **h** by i = 4% per day, a percentage that is applied each day on the previous day's total. Determine the product's size A after:

A) d = 2 days, with h = 8 m.

$$\underline{\hspace{6cm}}\ h$$
$$\underline{\hspace{6cm}}\ h+0.04*h = h(1+0.04)$$
$$\underline{\hspace{6.5cm}}\ h(1+0.04)+0.04*h(1+0.04) =$$
$$= h(1+0.04)(1+0.04)$$

Resolution: A = [h*(100% + i)](100% + i) =
= 8(1 + 0.04)(1 + 0.04) = 8*1.04*1,04 = 8*1.0816 =
= 8.6528. Answer: A = 8.6528 m.

B) d = 1 day, with h = 9 m. C) d = 2 days, with h = 20 m. D) d = 3 days, with h = 84 cm. E) d = 4 days, with h = 2 m.

To construct the amount formula for compound interest, we see that in each period we put in evidence 100%+i, or 1+i. If the time is in days, after two days we will have two parentheses (1+i), after three days, we will have three parentheses (1+i), and so on. Thus, if the time is **t** periods, we will have the parenthesis (1+i) raised to the power **t**, all starting from the capital C originally applied.

Our amount formula will then be:

$$A = C(1+i)^t$$

Exercise **P1.09**

With capital C applied at compound interest at rate i = 2% per month (p. m.), Determine the amount for a time of **t** months.

A) C = $700, t = 3 months.

Resolution: $A = C(1+i)^t = 700(1+0.02)^3 = 700*1.02^3 = 700*1.061208 = 742.8456$. Answer: A = 742.85. Note: (a) power must be calculated before multiplication; (b) do not round before the time!

B) C = $1,100, t = 2 months. C) C = $1,500, t = 3 months. D) C = $350, t = 4 months. E) C = $10,000, t = 1 month.

Exercise **P1.10**

An investor invested capital of $6,000, at compound interest at rate **i**, for **t** years. Determine the amount in the cases below.

A) i = 1% per annum, t = 5 years.

Resolution: $A = C(1+i)^t = 6000(1+0.01)^5 = 6000*1.01^5 = 6000*1.0510100501 = 6306.0603006$. Answer: A = $6,306.06. (Note that the increase, 306.06, interest on capital of 6000, is compatible with the rate i = 1% p.a. in order of magnitude.)

B) i = 2% p.a., t = 4 years. C) i = 3% p.a., t = 2 years. D) i = 5% p.a., t = 4 years. E) i = 2% p.a., t = 3 years.

Exercise **P1.11**

An investor has a capital C to invest for 4 months in a bank that pays compound interest rate **i**. Calculate the amount in each case.

A) C = $500, i = 3.5% p.m.

Resolution: $A = C(1+i)^t = 500(1+0{,}035)^4 = 500*1{,}035^4 = 500*1.147523000625 = 573.7615003125$.

Answer: A = $573.76.

B) C = $300, i = 5% p.m. C) C = $850, i = 2.5% p.m. D) C = $1.000, i = 1.5% p.m. E) C = $900, i = 2% p.m.

Exercise **P1.12**

Applied a given capital C, at an interest rate **i**, for 2 months, determine the value of C in the cases below knowing that the amount obtained was A = $1200.

A) i = 5% p.m.

Resolution: $A = C(1+i)^t \Leftrightarrow 1200 = C(1+0.05)^2 \Leftrightarrow 1200 = C*1.05^2 \Leftrightarrow 1200/1.05^2 = C \Leftrightarrow C = 1200/1.1025 = 1088.435374...$ Answer: $C \approx \$1,088.44$.

B) i = 2% p.m. C) i = 4% p.m. D) i = 6% p.m. E) i = 1% p.m.

Exercise **P1.13**

A capital of $800 was applied at an interest rate **i**, for 2 months. Determine the value of the rate **i** by knowing the amount obtained in the cases below.

A) A = $2400.

Resolution: $A = C(1+i)^t \Leftrightarrow 2400 = 800(1+i)^2 \Leftrightarrow 2400/800 = (1+i)^2 \Leftrightarrow 3 = (1+i)^2 \Leftrightarrow (1+i)^2 = 3 \Leftrightarrow 1+i = \sqrt{3} \Leftrightarrow 1+i \approx 1.73205... \Leftrightarrow i \approx -1 + 1.73205... = 0.73205...$ Answer: $i \approx 73.21\%$. (Note: in this exercise the student is authorized to use a calculator.)

B) A = $1200 C) A = $1600 D) A = $1000 E) A = $3000

Supplementary exercises

S1.01

For three days in a row a tree that was 2 meters tall grew 4% a day. Obtain the total value of this increase in meters. How much percent did the tree grow in those three days?

S1.02

Pinocchio lent Ali Baba all his coins, worth $200, at simple interest of 8% per month, for 11 months. Calculate the interest and the amount that Pinocchio should receive at the end of the period.

S1.03

Julia borrowed a capital of $3000, at simple interest of 2% per month, to pay in installments for 10 months. Determine the interest and the amount.

S1.04

A parts manufacturer had to cash a duplicate of face value n = $6,000, 20 days in advance, at the bank. Since the interest rate is 4% per month, determine the current value of the document.

S1.05

A merchant cashed at the bank a duplicate of face value $4,800 at 3% interest per month, receiving $4,200 as the current value. Find the anticipation deadline **p**.

S1.06

A man started training in running, always for the same daily time, having won on the first day 20 m. From the second day onwards, he always advanced 2% in increase compared to the previous day. Calculate how much percent he increased his performance until the fourth day and how many meters he ran that day.

S1.07

A client invested in the bank a capital C = $10,000, at the rate of i = 1% per month, in compound interest. Get the amount after three months.

S1.08

A citizen invested \$10,000 at compound interest of 3% p.a., for 4 years. Get the amount achieved.

S1.09

Mark lent a friend the sum of \$9,000, at compound interest of 4% per annum. Determine the amount after four years.

S1.10

Lucretius invested capital C for three years, at compound annual interest of 5%, and obtained an amount of \$8,740. Find out what was the capital C invested.

S1.11

Euclid invested a capital C = \$8,000 for two months, at monthly compound interest i, obtaining an amount of A = \$8,405. Find out the monthly rate i.

Chapter 2 - Interest yield time

In the previous chapter, we obtained, with the formula of amount for compound interest, values for capital, amount and interest rate. For interest rates we had to do root calculations. If we want to calculate application time at compound interest, we have to use a more advanced feature, which is the logarithm technique.

Obviously, in practice we have ready tables, which provide us with the values, but if the employee, the investor or the borrower has not studied logarithms, he will be working in the dark on this issue. It is good to know what is behind the results, especially in the financial market.

Exponential function

The logarithmic function is the inverse of the exponential function, which is simpler, so we start with this one.

An inverse function of $y = f(x)$ is a function $x = f(y)$. This means that the x-values of the starting set (domain) switch places with the y-values of the finishing set (codomain).

It is only possible to build an inverse function when the original function is injective, that is, each value **y** of the arrival set has only one corresponding **x** in the domain. Thus, the function $y = x^2$ is not injective, because when **x** is worth 2 the result **y** is $(2)^2$, which gives 4, but when **x** is worth -2, $(-2)^2$ also gives 4, so we have two departure values giving only one arrival, which is 4.

However, if there are infinite non-injective functions ($y = x^2$, $y = |x|$, $y = x^t$...) there are also infinite injective functions, such as $y = x$, $y = x^3$, $y = 6x$, $y = \log(x)$ e $y = \tan(x)$. (Note: $\log(x)$ is logarithm of **x** and $\tan(x)$ is tangent of **x**).

In addition to being injective, with each **y** being the result of an **x** that must be unique, to be reversible the function must also be surjective, or it must be adjusted to act as such. Surjective is a function that leaves no element of the finish set unused. If we take into account that the codomain of $y = x^2$ is the set of all real numbers, positive and negative, then it is not surjective, because no result will be negative, leaving unused all this region of the numerical line. But the function $y = x^3$ is surjective in the reals, because, for example, $(2)^3$ gives 8 and $(-2)^3$ gives -8.

The set of values effectively used by the function in the codomain is called the image-set, or simply Image.

We can now define the exponential function.

Exponential function is the function $y = f(x)$ given by $f(x) = a^x$, with **x** being any value of the real line, but the base **a** being valid only for positive reals discounting the number 1, that is, $a \in R_+ -\{1\}$.

The base **a** is neither domain nor codomain, but only one element in the construction of the function. Note that if the value is 1, the result will be a constant value, $y = 1$, not an exponential curve. And the exclusion of the negative region of the line in it occurs for several reasons, one of them being the need to make it reversible. Taking only positive values for **a**, the result $y = a^x$ will always be positive, even if **x** is negative, which will be very useful later on.

We should also note that when **a** is greater than 1, the function will be *increasing* (i. e., each time we take a larger number on the x-value side, we get a larger number on the y-value side) and when **a** is between 0 and 1, the function will be *decreasing*, i. e., has values decreasing as x-values increase, and vice versa. For example, in the function $y = (1/2)^x$, which has a base less than 1, doing $x = 2$ will result in 1/4, but increasing the value of x to 3, we will have result 1/8, which is half of previous.

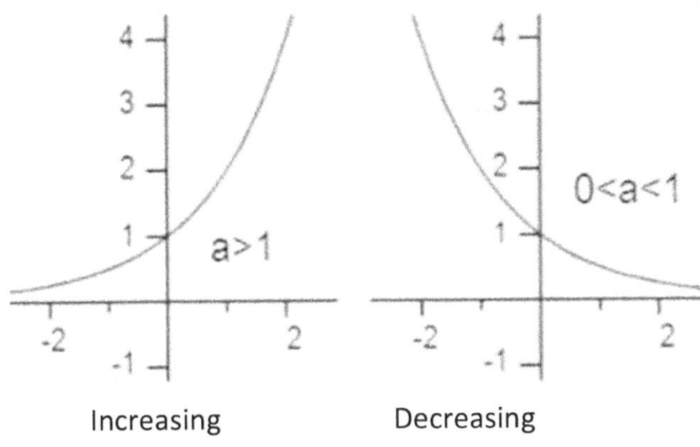

(The exponential function)

Exercise **P2.01**

Calculate the result **y** for three values of the domain, 1, 2, and 3, in each exponential function below.

A) $y=3^x$.

Resolution:

$f(1) = 3^1 = 3,$

$f(2) = 3^2 = 3*3 = 9,$

$f(3) = 3^3 = 3*3*3 = 27.$

B) $y=2^x$ C) $y=4^x$ D) $y=(1/2)^x$ E) $y=(3/2)^x$

Exercise **P2.02**

Applying three increasing values of x, -1, 0 and +1, check whether the given function is increasing or decreasing.

A) $y=(1/3)^x$

Resolution:

$f(-1) = (1/3)^{-1}=(3)^1 = 3,$

$f(0) = (1/3)^0=1,$

$f(1) = (1/3)^1 = 1/3.$ The function is decreasing.

Note: This type of verification is valid only for monotonic

functions, i. e., those that always increase or decrease always.
B) $y=2^x$ C) $y=3^x$ D) $y=(1/2)^x$ E) $y=(4/3)^x$

Exponential equation

While knowing that the exponential function is injective, we can solve equations whose members are exponential functions simply by comparing the arguments. For example, if 2^x is equal to 2^k, then **x** must be equal to **k**, since each value of **y** results from a unique value of **x**.

It is important to remember the fundamental properties of power, which are valid for exponential function: (i) power of the sum: $a^{x+y} = (a^x)*(a^y)$, (ii) power of difference: $a^{x-y} = (a^x):(a^y)$, (iii) power of power: $(a^x)^y = a^{x*y}$, (iv) power of negative: $a^{-n} = (1/a)^n$, (v) power of fraction (p-th root of a^n): $a^{n/p} = \sqrt[p]{(a^n)}$.

Take the example below. Write as single power, with positive exponent, the values: (a) $(3^5)*(3^4)$, (b) $(5^8):(5^2)$, (c) $(2^5)^3$, (d) 3^{-4}, (e) $\sqrt{(7^3)}$, (f) $(3/4)^{-6}$, (g) $(1/10)^{-3}$. As there is no specific exercise below to review these seven properties, it is advisable to pay close attention, in the next paragraph, to the results for these examples.

The solutions will be: (a) $3^{5+4} = 3^9$, (b) $5^{8-2} = 5^6$, (c) $2^{5*3} = 2^{15}$, (d) $(1/3)^4$, (e) $\sqrt{(7^3)} = 7^{3/2}$, (f) $(4/3)^6$, (g) 10^3.

Exercise P2.03
Solve each exponential equation below.
A) $3^{x+2} = 3^{5-4x}$
Resolution (by cutting the base value, 3, we just match the values of the exponents):

$$3^{x+2} = 3^{5-4x}$$
$$x+2 = 5-4x$$
$$x+4x = 5-2$$
$$5x = 3$$
$$x = 3/5. \quad S = \{3/5\}.$$

B) $2^{2x+1} = 2^{x-7}$ C) $5^{3-x} = 5^{7-2x}$ D) $2^{2x} = 2^5$ E) $7^{x^2-9x} = 7^{-20}$

Logarithmic function

Logarithmic function $y = \log_a x$ is the function **y** such that $a^y = x$, with **x** belonging to the full real line, but the base belonging to the positive reals discounting the value 1, i. e., $x \in R$, $a \in R_+$-$\{1\}$.

The value that is now **y**, in logarithms, was the value of **x** in the exponential function, and vice versa. Domain and Image have changed positions, but the base **a** remains in the same place, with the same possible values.

To calculate a given logarithm using the definition, we use the inverse function, working only with the exponential form.

Exercise **P2.04**
Calculate the logarithms below, by definition.
A) $\log_2 16$.
Resolution:

$$\log_2 16 = y \Leftrightarrow 2^y = 16$$
$$2^y = 16 \text{ (note: we will factor 16 into base 2)}$$
$$2^y = 2^4$$
$$y = 4.$$

B) $\log_2 32$ C) $\log_3 9$ D) $\log_5 125$ E) $\log_2(1/8)$

The whole theory of logarithms fits in the fingers of a hand. Calculating logarithm means calculating the exponent for a given power, but it all boils down to: a definition, as above, i. e., $y = \log_a x \Leftrightarrow a^y = x$, with due restrictions for base **a**, and four properties, which come as a result of the power properties. They are:

(1st) logarithm of product: $\log_a(x*y) = \log_a x + \log_a y$,
(2nd) logarithm of quotient: $\log_a(x/y) = \log_a x - \log_a y$,
(3rd) logarithm of power: $\log_a(x^p) = p*\log_a x$,
(4th) change of base: $\log_b x = \log_a x / \log_a b$.

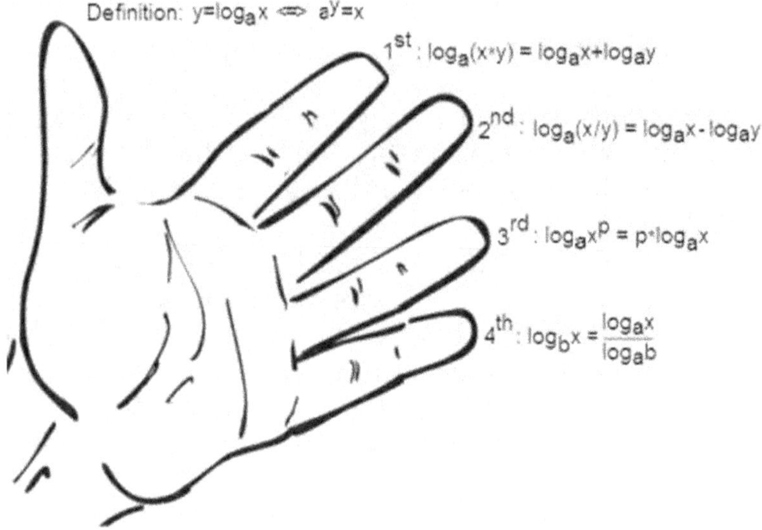

The role of properties is to facilitate work, often by providing shortcuts. With the 1st property we can "break" the logarithm of a value in the logarithms of the factors of that value. The same goes for the 2nd property in relation to the division's components. By the 3rd property, instead of calculating the property of a power, we can simply calculate the logarithm of its base and multiply the result by the exponent. The 4th property, which many find of little use, on the contrary, is of great importance, as it allows us to pass any logarithm to a given base, which is almost always base 10. The tables of logarithm are almost always on that base, for the so-called decimal logarithms. If someone asks us to calculate the approximate value, for example, of $\log_5 7$, we can change this base from 5 to 10 and look up the value in the table. The base 10 logarithms are so special that they do not need to have written the number 10 in place of the base. So $\log_{10} x$ is written as logx, and everyone will know that the base is 10.

In the same way that in the exponential function, the logarithmic function of base **a** greater than 1 is *increasing,* while with base **a** between 0 and 1, 0<a<1, it is *decreasing*.

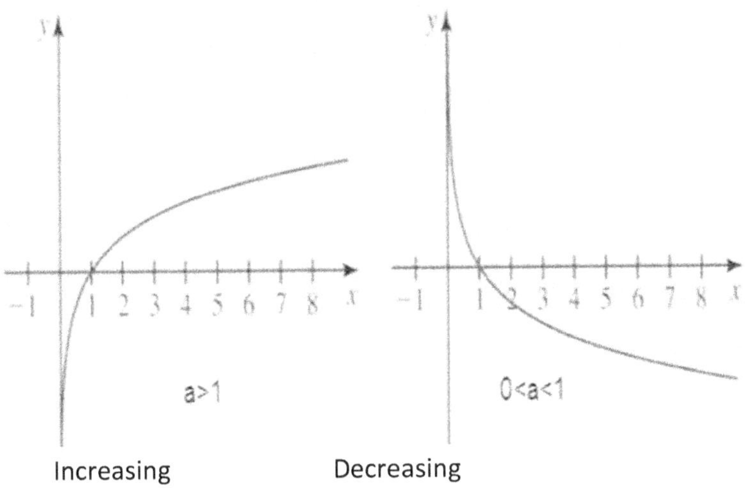

(*The logarithmic function*)

We can also easily demonstrate four basic facts that are very useful when dealing with logarithms: (a) $\log_a 1 = 0$, (b) $\log_a a = 1$, (c) $\log_a x = \log_a y \Leftrightarrow x=y$, e (d) $a^{\log_a(x)} = x$.

With that, we saw that logarithm of the unit is 0, logarithm of the base is 1, logarithm is an injective function and, finally, the base raised to the logarithm is equal to the argument.

Mantissa. The value of a base ten logarithm, which is usually obtained from a table, or from a calculator, consists of an entire part, before the dot, and a "broken" part. The whole value is called a *characteristic*, while the decimal part, which comes after the dot, is called *mantissa*.

In the expression $\log 1850 \approx 3.26717$, the characteristic is 3 and the mantissa is 0.26717. A mantissa is a non-negative value. If the value of a decimal logarithm is negative, the section that is before the dot is not the characteristic and the section that is after the dot is not yet the mantissa. We have to apply a little trick to get them.

For example, log0.028 ≈ -1.55284. How much are the characteristic and mantissa of this logarithm worth?

What we have is -1 + (-0.55284). To find the mantissa, we add 1 to this decimal part, which is in parentheses. So that the value of the logarithm is not changed, we add -1 to the number, but now in the whole part.

Thus, log0.026 ≈ -1-1 + (+ 1.0 - 0.5528) = -2+ (0.44716).

The characteristic is -2 and the mantissa is 0.44716. This operation is important in case we want to discover the argument of a logarithm when what is given to us is the final value of it.

Query. A table of decimal logarithms generally consists of a first column of two-digit numbers and ten columns of mantissas, without the initial dot, which is implied. At the top of the ten columns of mantissas there are numbers from 0 to 9 (**page 145**).

What does that mean?

That first two-digit number column is the column of the arguments, the values of **x**, or **n**. But we are not limited to two-digit numbers, once the ten digits above the columns of mantissas are complementary to the first column. If we take argument 23 in the first column, we can move to the right to, for example, the sixth column of mantissas. Above it is the digit 5 (counting starts with the digit 0). So we are looking at the intersection of this line 23 with the column above the digit 5 for the decimal logarithm of 2.53. Yes, once we understand mantissas starting with a dot, the numbers of the arguments in the first column are understood as values between 1.0 and 9.9, that is, values with a dot after the first digit.

For example, how much is log6.92 worth? We look at line 69 of the table and go to the right, going through column 0 and column 1, fixing our sight on column 2. We will find the mantissa .84011. Thus, $\log 6.92 \approx 0.84011$.

We are now very able at locating logarithms of values between 1.00 and 9.99 in the table. How do we find out logarithms of arguments outside this range?

Scientific. Here is one of the great advantages of using the table instead of a simple calculator. To use the table we are led to practice the scientific notation of numbers, while the calculator offers us the ready value, without requiring any reasoning from us other than the one involved in pressing the keys.

If we look at the $\log 430$ in a calculator, we will receive an approximate value of 2.63347. In the table, we already know how to find $\log 4.3$. So how to get to $\log 430$?

We simply write $\log 430 = \log(4.3*10^2)$. As the dot "moved" two places to the left of 430, reducing this coefficient in two orders, we add the exponent 2 to the power of 10.

We will have: $\log 430 = \log(4.3*10^2) = \log 4.3 + \log 10^2 = \log 4.3 + 2\log 10 = \log 4.3 + 2$.

(We used above property 1, property 3 and the fact that $\log_a a = 1$.)

Now just go to the table: $\log 430 = \log 4.30 + 2 \approx 0.63347 + + 2 = 2.63347$.

And for an argument less than 1, how do we do it?

Let's look for the value of $\log 0.00783$.

We have: $\log 0.00783 = \log(7.83*10^{-3})$. Here, the dot "walked" to the right, three places, increasing the value of the coefficient, which means that we had to decrease by 3, from 0 to -3, the exponent of the power of 10.

Finally:

$\log 0.00782 = \log(7.83*10^{-3}) = \log 7.83 + (-3)\log 10 \approx$ $\approx 0.89376 + (-3) = -2.10624$.

(In the logarithm above, the characteristic is -3 and the mantissa is 0.8938, but after the addition operation has been done with these two plots, the digits are different.

Characteristic and mantissa are preserved in the positive logarithms, as in the previous example, but do not in logarithms with a negative result.)

Exercise **P2.05**
Write as logarithm of a single number the decimal logarithms below.
A) $\log 35 - \log 7$
Resolution: $\log 35 - \log 7 = \log(35/7) = \log 5$. (Prop. 2nd)
B) $\log 20 - \log 5$. C) $\log 7 + \log 11$. D) $\log 30 - \log 6$. E) $\log 4 + \log 9 - \log 12$.

Exercise **P2.06**
Taking into account that $\log_a a = 1$, and $\log_a 1 = 0$, calculate the value of the logarithms below, using the 3rd property.
A) $\log_3 9$.
Resolution: $\log_3 9 = \log_3 3^2 = 2 * \log_3 3 = 2 * 1 = 2$.
B) $\log_5 25$ C) $\log_3 27$ D) $\log_7 7^8$ E) $\log_2 64$

Exercise **P2.07**
Write in terms of logarithms of decimal base each logarithm given below.
A) $\log_9 5$.
Resolution: $\log_9 5 = \log 5 / \log 9$ (prop. 4th)
B) $\log_5 11$ C) $\log_2 3$ D) $\log_7 2$ E) $\log_3 19$

Exercise **P2.08**
Calculate, using the table, with $x < 10$, the decimal logarithms below.
A) $\log 14$.
Resolution: $\log 14 = \log 2 + \log 7 \approx 0.30103 + 0.84510 = = 1.14610$.
B) $\log 35$ C) $\log 15$ D) $\log 64$ (prop. 3[a]) E) $\log 21$ F) $\log 81$.

Exercise **P2.09**
Obtain the fraction that represents the approximate value of the given logarithm.
A) $\log_7 8$.
Resolution: $\log_3 8 = \log 8 / \log 7 \approx 0.90309/0.84510 =$
$= 90309/84511$ (Note: Prop. 4th).
B) $\log_9 7$ C) $\log_2 7$ D) $\log_5 3$ E) $\log_4 9$

Exercise **P2.10**
Calculate the value of the following decimal logarithms.
A) $\log(10/7)$.
Resolution: $\log(10/7) = \log 10 - \log 7 \approx 1.0 - 0.84510 =$
$= 0.15490$ (Note: $\log_a a = 1$).
B) $\log(10/3)$ C) $\log(1/7)$ D) $\log(100/9)$ E) $\log(2/5)$ F) $\log(1/30)$

Exercise **P2.11**
Find the logarithm below in the table.
A) $\log 0.0587$.
Resolution:
$\log 0.0587 = \log[5.87*10^{-2}] = \log 5.87 + (-2)\log 10 \approx$
$\approx 0.76864 + (-2) = -1.23136$.
B) $\log 0.716$. C) $\log 47.2$. D) $\log 0.0023$. E) $\log 83000$.

Application time

The most common case of approximation of numbers for higher orders is rounding, but in certain cases we need to approach the ceiling ($y = ceil(x)$) or, also, the floor ($y = floor(x)$).
So, if we have to write 7.48 to the place of tenths, rounding up to 7.5. The floor is 7.4, while the ceiling is 7.5. If the value is 7.53, rounding is 7.5, the floor is 7.5, and the ceiling is 7.6.
If we are calculating the application time at compound interest, the approximation of the result, when necessary, must

be taken into account by the ceiling, otherwise, there will be no time to complete the income we are looking for.

If we want to know how long we have to keep invested a given capital to obtain a desired amount, we need to use logarithms, because of its 3rd property, which allows to "overturn" the exponent, transforming it into a mere factor.

Exercise **P2.12**

When investing a capital C = $500, find out the necessary number of months of investment to obtain the amount A, at an interest rate **i**.

A) A = $1000, i=3% p.m.

Resolution:

$A = C(1+i)^t$

$1000 = 500(1+0.03)^t$

$1000/500 = (1+0.03)^t$

$2 = 1.02^t$ (note: we will apply logarithm to both members)

$\log 2 = \log(1.03^t)$

$\log 2 = t*\log(1.03)$ (for the 3rd property)

$0.30103 \approx t*0.01284$ (table value - end of book)

$t \approx 0.30103/0.01284 = 30103/1284 \approx 23.49922$. Answer: t = 24 months.

B) A = $1000, i=2% p.m. C) M = $750, i=4% p.m. D) A = $1500, i=5% p.m. E) A = $800, i=2% p.m.

Exercise **P2.13**

We have available capital and we want to invest a certain amount so that within **t** years, at compound interest **i**, we will reach an amount of at least $4000. Obtain the required number of years **t**, in whole value.

A) C = $2000, i = 4% p.a.

Resolution:

$M = C(1+i)^t$

$4000 = 2000(1+0.04)^t$

$$4000/2000 = (1+0.04)^t$$
$$2 = 1.04^t$$
$$\log 2 = \log(1.04^t)$$
$$\log 2 = t{*}\log(1.04)$$
$$0.30103 \approx t{*}0.01703$$
$$t \approx 0.30103/0.01703 = 30103/1703 \approx 17.67645...$$

Answer: t = 18 years.

B) C = \$2500, i = 3% p.a. C) C = \$3200, i = 2% p.a. D) C = \$1000, i = 6% p.a. E) C = \$2352.94, i = 4% p.a.

Exercise **P2.14**

An investor invested \$800 and obtained an amount A after 4 months. Determine the monthly interest rate **i** in the cases below.

A) A = \$848.

Resolution:

$$A = C(1+i)^t$$
$$848 = 800(1+i)^4$$
$$848/800 = (1+i)^4$$
$$1.06 = (1+i)^4$$
$$\log 1.06 = \log[(1+i)^4]$$
$$0.02531 \approx 4{*}\log(1+i)$$
$$\log(1+i) = 0.02531/4$$
$$\log(1+i) = 0.0063 \text{ (we'll get the closest one: 0.0065)}$$
$$i+i \approx 1.015$$
$$i = 1.015 - 1 = 0.015. \text{ Answer: } i = 1.5\%.$$

B) A = \$864. C) A = \$900. D) A = \$832. E) A = \$960

Table:

x	1.01	1.015	1.02	1.045	1.05	1.125	1.2
logx	.0043	.0065	.0086	.0191	.0212	.0512	.0791

Fisher Equation

So far we have been working with the interest rate **i**, which is the nominal rate. So, if the investor today invests an amount of \$1000 and 11 months from now he gets an amount of \$1140, we were considering that he earned \$140 in interest income. The situation referred to an ideal currency, without inflation.

In a market in which the currency is depreciated, which we call inflation, that income that the investor obtained is less than the \$140 that he would actually earn if inflation were zero.

To obtain the value of the real interest rate **r**, from the nominal interest rate **i**, while taking into account the expected inflation action, represented by the letter π, economist Irving Fisher developed in the early 20th century the relation we now call *Fisher Equation*.

$$1+i = (1+r)*(1+\pi)$$

For example, a customer has an amount of \$900 to invest for a year and wants to analyze the proposal from two different banks, bank A, which offers 20% nominal interest (**i**), and bank B, which offers 6% interest real interest (**r**) and the correction of inflation for the period. Which bank has the greatest advantage and in what situation?

$$1+i = (1+r)*(1+\pi)$$
$$900*(1+0.20) = 900*(1+0.06)*(1+\pi)$$
$$(1+0.06)*(1+\pi) = (1+0.20)$$
$$1+\pi = 1.20/1.06 \approx 1.132075...$$
$$\pi \approx 1.1321- 1.0 = 0.1321 = 13.21\%.$$

The conclusion is that bank B is more advantageous if inflation for the year is higher than 13.21%.

Exercise **P2.15**

The financial market pays 15% per annum of nominal interest rates, but a new bank offers to pay real interest rates, with inflation correction. Find out from which inflation rate of the year it is advisable to invest a given capital C in this new bank.

A) r = 4%.
Resolution:
$$1+i = (1+r)*(1+\pi)$$
$$C*(1+0.15) = C*(1+0.04)*(1+\pi)$$
$$(1+0.04)*(1+\pi) = (1+0.15)$$
$$1+\pi = 1.15/1.04 \approx 1.1057692...$$
$$\pi \approx 1.1058- 1.0 = 0.1058 = 10.58\%.$$
B) r = 3.5% C) r = 5% d) r = 3% E) r = 4.7%.

Exercise **P2.16**

If the expected inflation rate is 12% for the year in question, determining from which nominal interest rate offered by the market this can surpass the advantage of a bank that offers real interest **r**, with inflation correction.

A) r = 5%.
Resolution:
$$1+i = (1+r)*(1+\pi)$$
$$C*(1+i) = C*(1+0.05)*(1+0.12)$$
$$1+i = (1+0.05)*(1+0.12)$$
$$1+i = 1.05*1.12 = 1.176.$$
$$i = 1.176- 1.0 = 0.176 = 17.6\%.$$
B) r = 4.5% C) r = 3.5% d) r = 4% E) r = 4.2%.

Discreet rate and continuous rate

In the financial market, we are almost always dealing with a discrete interest rate, that is, a capitalized rate over a given period. But we can also determine the continuous interest rate, based on its relationship with the discrete rate:

$$Ic = \ln (1 + Id)$$

The formula says that the continuous rate, Ic, is the natural (or Neperian) logarithm of 1 plus the discrete rate Id.

Natural logarithm, $y = \ln(x)$, is the logarithm in the base e, Euler constant ($e = 2.1782818...$). So $y = \ln(x)$ is the same as $y = \log_e(x)$.

Using the inverse function of the logarithm, we can obtain the discrete rate from the continuous rate, with the formula:

$$Id = -1 + e^{Ic}$$

Let's look at an example.

If a given investment for interest rate $i = 0.5\%$ per month, discrete rate, what will be the equivalent continuous rate?

We have:

$Id = 0.005$

$Ic = \ln(1 + 0.005) = \ln(1.005) \approx 0.004987544$

The continuous interest rate is therefore $Ic = 0.4987544\%$.

What will be the continuous rate equivalent to the discrete rate $Id = 25\%$ per annum?

We have: $Ic = \ln(1 + 0.25) = \ln(1.25) \approx 0.2231436$.

The equivalent continuous rate is $Ic = 22.31436\%$

We see that the value of the continuous rate is always slightly less than that of the discrete rate.

For the rate $Ic = 0.4987544\%$, we calculate the equivalent discrete rate.

We have:

$Id = -1 + e^{0.004987544} = -1 + 1.0050000025 \approx 0.005 = 0.5\%$.

To find the real interest rate, while considering the inflation rate, using the continuous rate or the discrete rate, in order to avoid "monetary illusion", we do:

$r = i - \pi$, for continuous rate.

$1+r = (1 + i)/(1+ \pi)$, for discrete rate.

(This second formula is the Fisher equation, which we saw above.)

Exercise **P2.17**

Find out the continuous rate equivalent to the given monthly discrete rate.

A) i = 3%.

Resolution:

Ic = ln(1+0.03) = ln(1.03) ≈ 0.0295588

Answer: Ic = 2.95588%.

B) i = 0.2%. C) i = 6%. D) i = 0.08%. E) i = 10%.

Net present value

The *present value* P in an investment that corresponds to capital C, considering the moment when the investment is made. The expected amount A is, therefore, the *future value*, F.

The formula for the future value is therefore the same as for the amount:

$$F = P*(1+i)^t$$

P|________________ t
               | F Future value: capitalization.

For the present value, just isolate the value P:

$$P = \frac{F}{(1+i)^t}$$

P|________________ t   Present value: discount.
            | F

If we have a cash flow producing a given value, it will be seen as *net present value*, Npv, which is the sum of the various present values:

$$Npv = -Io + \sum \frac{Ct}{(1+r)^t}$$

(Io is investment value.)

```
        C1   C2   C3        Ct
       __|____|____| ... ___|
Npv |
```

For an example, suppose that a bank offers us a plan in which we invest \$100,000 over four years, at a discount rate **r** of 2% p.a., with earnings of \$10,000, \$20,000, \$50,000 and \$60,000 in successive years. What will be the net present value?

```
        10000    20000  50000  60000
       _______|_______|_______|_______|
       |
   100000
```

We have:

$$Npv = -Io + \sum \frac{Ct}{(1+r)^t} = -Io + C1/(1+r)^1 + C2/(1+r)^2 + ...$$

$+Ct/(1+r)^t$

So we will have:

$Npv = -100000 + 10000/(1+0.02)^1 + 20000/(1+0.02)^2 +$
$+50000/(1+0.02)^3 + 60000/(1+0.02)^4 =$
$= -100000 + 10000/1.02^1 + 20000/1.02^2 + 50000/1.02^3 +$
$+60000/1.02^4 \approx -100000 + 10000/1.02 + 20000/1.0404 +$
$+ 50000/1.061208 + 60000/1.082432 \approx -100000+9803.920 +$
$+ 19223.376 + 47116.117 + 55430.733 = -100000 + 131574.146 =$
$= 31574.146$

$Npv \approx \$31,574.15$

The net present value will be \$31,574.15, which is a positive number, thus representing a gain for the investor.

One of the most common uses of calculating net present value is when comparing different types of investments. Two banks offer us plans to invest in them. By obtaining the net present value of each of the two cases, we can easily decide which offer is most advantageous.

To obtain a given power in the table, in approximate value, just use a property of the logarithmic function and its injectivity condition. For example, to find 1.02^3, we do:

$$logx = log1.02^3 = 3*log1.02 \approx 3*0,00860 = 0.0258.$$

Now just look for that mantissa and see what value of **x** (in the first column followed by the complement) provides it. We see that it is on line 10 under column 6, so that:

$$log1.06 \approx log1.02^3 \Leftrightarrow 1.02^3 \approx 1.06.$$

We could have done all the powers, therefore, through the table, but we would lose a lot of precision, due to drastic rounding. That is why we prefer to suggest to the student, without prejudice to learning, to obtain the negative exponent power directly from the financial calculator - with the power taken to the numerator -, taking a convenient approximation, which in this case involved six digits after the comma.

We must remember that the financial calculator does all the calculation of net present value automatically, just by feeding it with the data. But, if the student does not solve the problem step by step, as in this example, he will have no way of knowing what the calculator is doing. He will be its servant, not the other way around.

Exercise **P2.18**

An investor applies a certain amount P, at interest of 4% p.a., for 3 years, hoping to reach an amount F, future value. Determine the present value P in the cases below.

A) F = $1012.38.

Resolution:

$$P = \frac{F}{(1+i)^t}$$

P = 1012.38/[(1+0.04)³] = 1012.38/(1.04³) =
= 1012.38/1.124864 ≈ 900.00

Answer: P ≈ $900.

B) F = $1237.36. C) F = $2000. D) F = $1800 E) F = = $1203.61

Exercise **P2.19**

A bank offers investors a plan in which, against a deposit of $10,000, it pays a discount rate (or IRR, internal rate of return) **r** of 4% p.a., market rate, for three years. Obtain the net present value for the surrender values given below for the first, second and third years, respectively.

A) $2000, $4000 and $6000.

Resolution:

$$Npv = -Io + \sum \frac{Ct}{(1+r)^t}$$

Npv = -Io + C1/(1+r)¹+C2/(1+r)²+Ct/(1+r)³.

Npv =

=-10,000+2000/(1+0.04)¹+4000/(1+0.04)²+6000/(1+0.04)³=
= -10.000 + 2000/1,04¹ + 4000/1,04² + 6000/1,04³ =
= -10,000 + 2000/1.04 + 4000/1.0816 + 6000/1.124864 =
= -10,000 + 1923.076923 + 3698.224852 + 5333.978152 ≈
≈ -10,000 + 10,955.28 = 955.28.

Npv ≈ $955.28. a positive gain for the customer.

B) $1000, $4000 and $8000. C) $2000, $5000 and $6000. D) $3000, $4000 and $5500. E) $2000, $5000 and $6400.

Exercise **P2.20**

In a market that pays a 3% p.a. rate of return, a given bank offers a customer who has $30,000 to invest surrenders in the first and second years that result in a net present value of

$3,443.30. Of the other banks below, which offer the surrenders below, decide which ones guarantee the highest income for the customer and which ones yield the least.

A) $15,000 e $20,000.

Resolution:

$Npv = -Io + C1/(1+r)^1 + C2/(1+r)^2$.

$Npv = -30000 + 15000/1.03^1 + 20000/1.03^2 =$

$= -30000 + 15000/1.03 + 20000/1.0609 \approx$

$\approx -30000 + 14563.107 + 18851.918 =$

$= -30000 + 33415.025 \approx 3415.025$.

$Npv \approx \$3,415.03$. A lower yield.

B) $16,000 and $19,000. C) $17,000 and $18,000. D) $14,000 and $22,000. E) $14,000 and $21,000

Supplementary exercises

S2.01

For the values 1, 2 and 4 of the domain, obtain each result y of the exponential function $y = 5^{-2}$.

S2.02

Manuel has capital C to invest in a bank that pays an annual rate. If he makes the investment for 3 years, he will get an amount of $21,854.54. If he only invests for 2 years, the amount will be $21,218. What is the value of capital C and what is the interest rate **i**?

(Note: The student will have a multiplicative system, so just put the first equation over the second and simplify.)

S2.03

Solve the exponential equation $(1/2)^{7-2x} = (1/2)^{4x-5}$.

S2.04

Calculate, by using the definition, the logarithms below.

a) $\log_2 64$ b) $\log_3 81$ c) $\log_{(1/5)} 5$.

S2.05
Write as logarithm of a single number each logarithm below.
a) $\log 2 + \log 6$ b) $\log 33 - \log 11$ c) $\log 2 + \log 6 - \log 3$

S2.06
Calculate the logarithms below using the 3rd property.
a) $\log_3 243$ b) $\log_5 25$ c) $\log_{11} 121$

S2.07
Write in the form of base 10 logarithms each logarithm below.
a) $\log_5 7$ b) $\log_{11} 3$ c) $\log_{13} 12$ d) $\log_3 2$

S2.08
By using the table values for $x < 10$, calculate the logarithms below.
a) $\log 6$ b) $\log 12$ c) $\log 45$ d) $\log 24$

S2.09
Give the fraction that represents the approximation of the logarithm.
a) $\log_3 7$ b) $\log_5 7$ c) $\log_2 5$ d) $\log_{11} 3$

S2.10
By using the 2nd property, calculate each decimal logarithm below.
a) $\log(3/10)$ b) $\log(7/5)$ c) $\log(5/3)$ d) $\log(7/9)$

S2.11
Obtain, by using the table, each logarithm below.
a) $\log 0.00356$ b) $\log 85400$ c) $\log 0.0149$ d) $\log 9420000$

S2.12

For an investment of C = $1,200, at compound interest of 0.4% per month, find out the necessary whole number of months so that the amount is at least A = $1,600.

S2.13

Find the entire whole of years so that a capital C = = $10,000, applied at 4% interest per annum, produces an amount of at least $ 13,000.

S2.14

Find out the compound monthly interest rate i, so that a capital of $6,000, applied over five months, leads to an amount of $7,200.

S2.15

A bank pays investors a nominal interest rate of 10% per annum. A new bank offers a real annual rate of 8%. Find out what annual inflation rate is worth investing in the new bank.

S2.16

The expected inflation in a given year is 8%. A certain bank pays interest at a real rate r = 4%, with inflation adjustment. Calculate from what nominal rate the other bank can offer the client a better proposal than this.

S2.17

Calculate what value of the continuous rate is equivalent to the discrete monthly rate i = 2%.

S2.18

Marcelo invested a sum P, with interest of 3% p.a., hoping to reach, in 5 years, a future value F = $5,900. Find out the amount applied.

S2.19

An investor makes a deposit of $8,000 in a plan that pays a rate of return r = 5% p.a. Obtain the net present value for the surrender amounts of $4,200 and $4,600, respectively, in the first and second years.

S2.20

Moses intends to invest in a bank A, which pays a rate r = 4% p.a., the amount of $16,000, intending to make surrenders of $9,000 and $8,000 in the following two years. Another bank, B, at the same rate, suggests surrenders of $8,000 and $9,200. Checking the net present value in both cases, deciding which of the two banks offers Moses the greatest advantage.

Chapter 3 - Simple annuities

An *annuity* is every sequence of equal periodic payments. There are many types of annuities, but in this book we will deal only with the right ordinary annuities. The time between one payment and the next is called the *payment interval.*

An annuity is *simple* when the interest is calculated at a constant rate over each payment interval

An annuity is said to be *right* when payments have set dates to be made. The opposite of this is the contingent annuity, which takes place on dates that depend on events whose occurrence is not foreseen.

An annuity is *ordinary* when each payment is made at the end of the respective payment interval

Let us take as an example the case of a worker who authorizes the bank to deposit in his investment account a portion of \$100 per month of his salary, for 10 quarters (two and a half years), at 1% quarterly interest.

Let us see what happens with the account at the end of the 2.5 years.

After the first quarter, the amount in your account is $A9 = 100(1.01)^9$. For the second quarter, $A8 = 100(1.01)^8$ is added, following this sequence until in the eighth quarter there is $A1 = 100(1.01)^1$ and in the last, the ninth, $A0 = 1000(1.01)^0$.

<pre>
 | | | | | | | | |
 1   2   3   4   5   6   7   8   9
</pre>

We have:

$A = A0+A1+A2+...+A9 = 100(1+1.01+1.01^2+...+1.01^9)$.

The series in parentheses results in a geometric progression of 10 terms (n=10), with reason $q = 1.01$ and $a_1 = 1$.

Thus:

$S_n = a_1(1-q^n)/(1-q)$

S_9 = $1(1 - 1.01^{10})/(1-1.01) \approx (1-1.104622125)/(-0.01) =$
$= -0.104622125/(-0.01) = 10.4622125/1 \approx 10.4622$.

The final amount will be $A \approx \$100*10.4622 = \$1046.22$.

Without taking into account inflation or any other type of depreciation, we can calculate the present value of these payments.

Since the amount formula is $A = C(1+i)^t$, each amount of invested capital C brought to present value will be $C = = A/[(1+i)^t]$, or $C = A*(1 + i)^{-t}$.

For the first payment, that first installment of \$100, the present value is $C1 = 100*(1.01)^{-1}$. For the second installment we have $C2 = 100*(1.01)^{-2}$. While continuing with these accounts we arrive at the last installment, which has a present value $C10 = 100*(1.01)^{-10}$.

The sum of the successive present values, which will give the total present value P, or current value, will be:

$P = C_1 +C_2+C_3 +...+C_{10}$ = $100*[(1.01)^{-1}+(1.01)^{-2}+(1.01)^{-3}+...$
$+(1.01)^{-10}]$.

If we multiply the plots within the brackets by 1.01, we will form a geometric progression with $a_1 = 1$, $q = 1.01^{-1}$ (or $q = 1/1.01$) and $n = 10$.

Thus:

$P = (100/1.01)*[1+(1.01)^{-1}+(1.01)^{-2}+(1.01)^{-3}+...+(1.01)^{-9}]$

The sum of the series inside the brackets will be:

$a_1 = a_1(1 - q^n)/(1 - q)$

$S_{10} = 1[1 - 1.01^{-1*10}]/(1-1/1.01) \approx$

$\approx (1.0-0.905286955)/[(1.01-1.0)/1.01] \approx$

$\approx 0.094713045/(0.01/1.01)$.

We will have:

$P \approx (100/1.01)*0.094713045/(0.01/1.01) =$

$= 100*0.094713045/0.01 = 100*0.094713045/[100^{-1}] =$

= 100*0.094713045*100 = 10000*0.094713045 ≈ 947.13.

Thus, those 10 installments of $100 complete a present value of P = $947.13 (note that this is less than the simple product $100*10 and is equivalent to the real value of the money, at that interest rate, if it were being kept under the mattress).

Exercise **P3.01**

Take the case of a person who deposits for 1.5 years (six quarters), in an investment account that pays interest **i**, the same amount R, at the end of each quarter. Find out the amount reached at the end of the period, for the data below.

A) R = $80, i = 6% p.a. (6%/4 = 1.5% quarterly).

Resolution:

From what we saw above, the amount will be:

A = R*Sn.

In this exercise, n=6, a_1 = 1 e q = 1.015.

$S_n = a_1(1 - q^n)/(1 - q)$

S_6 = 1(1-1.015^6)/(1-1.015) ≈ (1 − 1.0934432639)/(- 0.015) =

= -0.0934432639/(-0.015) ≈ 6.229551.

A ≈ 80*6.229551

A ≈ 498.36.

B) R = $90, i = 8% p.a. C) R = $110, i = 4% p.a. D) R = $80, i = 8% p.a. E) R = $120, i = 6% p.a.

Exercise **P3.02**

Find out the present value in each of the investment situations of the previous year.

A) R = $80, i = 6% p.a.

Resolution:

We saw by the example above that:

P = [R/(1+i)]*Sn.

For this exercise, n = 6, a_1 = 1 e q = 1/(1+i).

We have:

$S_n = a_1(1 - q^n)/(1 - q)$

$S_6 = 1[1 - 1.015^{-6}]/(1-1/1.015) \approx$

$\quad \approx (1.0\text{-}0.914542193)/[(1.015\text{-}1.0)/1.015] \approx$

$\quad \approx 0.085458/(0.015/1.015).$

$P = (80/1.015)*0.085458/(0.015/1.015) =$

$\quad = 80*0.085458/0.015 \approx 5333.333*0.085458 \approx 455.78.$

B) R = \$90, i = 8% p.a. C) R = \$110, i = 4% p.a.. D) R = = \$80, i = 8% p.a. E) R = \$120, i = 6% p.a.

Annuity formulas

The value R, the amount paid at the end of each period of an annuity, is called *periodic payment*. It is also customary to use the $Vn\rceil i$ notation, which reads "V angle **n** at rate **i**", to denote the total present value of the annuity, and the $An\rceil i$ notation, which reads "A angle **n** at rate **i**", to denote the final amount in the annuity (instead of $Vn\rceil i$ and $An\rceil i$, $Pn\rceil i$ and $Sn\rceil i$ are also used).

We will build simpler formulas than the previous ones, although a little less intuitive.

Based on what we've studied so far,

$An\text{-}1 = R(1+i)^{n-1}, An\text{-}2 = R(1+i)^{n-2},...,$

$\quad A2 = R(1+i)^2, A1 = R(1+i)^1, Ao = R.$

We also have that:

$An\rceil i = Ao + A1 + A2 +...+ An\text{-}2 + An\text{-}1 =$

$\quad = R[1 + (1+i)^1 + (1+i)^2 +...+ (1+i)^{n-2} + (1+i)^{n-1}] =$

$\quad = R\{[1 - (1+i)^n]/[1 - (1+i)]\} = R\{[(1+i)^n - 1]/i\}.$

So,

$\quad An\rceil i = R\{[(1+i)^n - 1]/i\}.$

Or: $An\rceil i = Ran\rceil i$, if we call $[(1+i)^n - 1]/i$ as $an\rceil i$.

If the context does not give rise to confusion, we simply say:

$$A = R\frac{[(1+i)^n - 1]}{i}$$

For the sequence of the present values we do an analogous job.

We have:

$C_1 = R(1+i)^{-1}$, $C_2 = R(1+i)^{-2}$, ..., $C_{n-1} = R(1+i)^{-(n-1)}$, $C_n = R(1+i)^{-n}$.

$Pn\rceil i = C_1 + C_2 + ... + C_{n-1} + C_n =$
$= R\{(1+i)^{-1} + (1+i)^{-2} + ... + (1+i)^{-(n-1)} + (1+i)^{-n}\} =$
$= R(1+i)[1 - (1+i)^{-n}]/[1 - 1/(1+i)] = R[1 - (1+i)^{-n}]/i$.

So,

$Pn\rceil i = R[1 - (1+i)^{-n}]/i$.

Or: $Pn\rceil i = Rpn\rceil i$, if we call $[1 - (1+i)^{-n}]/i$ as $pn\rceil i$.

The student should note that in the formula for the future value A the exponent is **n**, while in the formula for the present value P, whose result is generally smaller, we have exponent -n.

Here too, in the absence of confusion as to the context, we write:

$$P = R\frac{[1-(1+i)^{-n}]}{i}$$

Exercise **P3.03**

A lady invests in a bank account for a year, at annual interest **i** compounded monthly, an annuity of value R, deposited at the end of each month. Find out the amount to be obtained in the cases below.

A) i = 6% p.a., R = $90.

Resolution:

Rate i = 6% p.a. with monthly capitalization it gives i = 0.5% p.m. Here, n = 12.

$A = R*[(1+i)^n - 1]/i$.

$A = 90*[(1.005)^{12} - 1]/0.005 \approx$
$\approx 90*[1.0616778 - 1]/0.005 =$
$= 90*0.0616778/0.005 = 90*12.33556 = 1110.2004$.

Answer: A = $1,110.20.

Note:

When we say compound interest "monthly", or "semi-annually", or "quarterly", we have to divide that rate given as annual by 12, by 6 or by 3. This is a simplification made for practical purposes, since compounding 0.5% for 12 months does not result in 6%, but at a higher rate: $i = (1 + 0.005)^{12} - 1 \approx$ $\approx 0.0617 = 6.17\%$.

B) i = 12% p.a., R = $100. C) i = 6% p.a., R = $120. D) i = = 6% p.a., R = $150. E) i = 12% p.a., R = $200.

Exercise **P3.04**

Find out the present value P for the account of the same lady from the previous year.

A) i = 6% p.a., R = $90.

Resolution:

We have: i = 0.5% p.m. and n = 12.

$P = R[1 - (1+i)^{-n}]/i$.

$P = 90[1 - (1.005)^{-12}]/0.005 \approx$

$\approx 90[1 - 0.9419053]/0.005 \approx$

$= 90*0.0580947/0.005 = 90*11.61894 = 1045.7046$.

Answer: P = $1045.70.

B) i = 12% p.a., R = $100. C) i = 6% p.a., R = $120. D) i = 6% p.a.., R = $150. E) i = 12% p.a., R = $200.

Exercise **P3.05**

A man invests for two years a capital R each quarter, in a bank with annual interest rates **i**, compounded quarterly. Obtain the present value and the amount in the cases below.

A) i = 8% p.a., R = $200.

Resolution:

We have: i = 8%/4 = 2% quarterly, and n = 8.

$P = R[1 - (1+i)^{-n}]/i$.

$P = 200[1 - (1,02)^{-8}]/0.02 \approx$

$\approx 200[1 - 0.8534904]/0.02 \approx$

$= 200*0.1465096/0.02 = 200*7.32548 = 1465.0960$.
For the amount:
$A = R[(1+i)^n - 1]/i$.
$A = 200*[(1.02)^8 - 1]/0.02 \approx$
$\approx 200*[1.1716594 - 1]/0.02 =$
$= 200*0.1716594/0.02 = 200*8.582970 = 1716.5940$.
Answer: $P = \$1,465.10$ e $A = 1,716.59$.
B) $i = 8\%$ p.a., $R = \$120$. C) $i = 6\%$ p.a., $R = \$240$. D) $i = 4\%$ p.a., $R = \$300$. E) $i = 6\%$ p.a., $R = \$160$.

Exercise **P3.06**

Anna Lucy decided to pay a debt by depositing monthly the amount C for **n** months with interest of 12% p.a. compounded monthly, plus a final payment of value F. Obtain the present value Pf of the debt for the cases below.

A) $C = \$80$, n = 11 months and $F = \$250$.
Resolution:
We have: $i = 12\%/12 = 1\%$ p.m., and n = 11.
$Pf = R[1 - (1+i)^{-n}]/i + F*(1+i)^{-n}$
$Pf = 80[1 - (1.01)^{-11}]/0.01 + 250[1.01^{-11}] \approx$
$\approx 80[1 - 0.8963237]/0.01 + 250*0.8963237 =$
$= 80*0.1036763/0.01 + 250*0.8963237 =$
$= 80*10.36763 + 250*0.8963237 =$
$= 829.4104 + 224.080925 = 1053.91325$.
Answer: The present value of the debt was $1,053.49.
B) $C = \$100$, n = 12 months and $F = \$120$. C) $C = \$90$, n = 10 months and $F = \$150$. D) $C = \$120$, n = 14 months and $F = \$200$. E) $C = \$110$, n = 9 months and $F = \$140$.

Supplementary exercises

S3.01
A man deposited the same amount of $400 for five years in a bank that paid 3% interest p.a. Find out the amount right after the fifth year deposit.

S3.02
Sara deposited the value R = $500 for eight years in a bank whose interest rate was 2% p.a. Give the amount and the present value in the eighth year.

S3.03
Julius bought a car by paying $900 down payment and agreeing to pay an annual rate of $200 each end of the month for 10 months, with interest of 6% p.a. composed monthly. Obtain the equivalent of the cash value of the car, that is, the present value. (Note: To P, present value, we must add the value of the entry, at the end of the account.)

S3.04
Cecilia started to pay a debt by depositing a fixed amount of $200 per month for 15 months, promising to pay off the entire commitment with a final payment of $140. While knowing that the interest charged is 2% per month, obtain the present value of the debt.

S3.05
A citizen contracted a debt whose contract provides for deposits of $120 monthly for 14 months, with interest of 18% p.a. composed monthly, plus a final payment of $350. Calculate the present value of that debt.

S3.06
John Peter wanted to pay a debt by depositing the amount of $50 per month for 13 months with interest of 12% p.a. composed monthly, plus a final payment of F = $300. Obtain the present value P of the debt.

Chapter 4 - Payments, deadline and interest on annuities

In the formulas $An_{\rceil}i = Ran_{\rceil}i$ and $Pn_{\rceil}i = Rpn_{\rceil}i$, from the previous chapter, we can isolate the payment R, called periodic payment, obtaining:

I) $R = A*1/an_{\rceil}i$ and

II) $R = P*1/pn_{\rceil}i$,

calling $An_{\rceil}i$ simply A and $Pn_{\rceil}i$ simply P.

So, in terms of A we have:

$$R = A*i/[(1+i)^n - 1]$$

and, in terms of P,

$$R = P*i/[1 - (1+i)^{-n}].$$

We can also show that:

$$1/an_{\rceil}i + i = 1/pn_{\rceil}i.$$

Let us see.

$1/an_{\rceil}i + i = 1/\{[(1+i)^n - 1]/i\} + i = i/[(1+i)^n - 1] + i =$

$= \{i + i[(1+i)^n - 1]\}/[(1+i)^n - 1] = i\{1 + [(1+i)^n - 1]\}/[(1+i)^n - 1] =$

$= i[(1+i)^n]/[(1+i)^n - 1] = i/\{[(1+i)^{-n}]*[(1+i)^n - 1]\} =$

$= i/\{[(1+i)^{-n}]*[(1+i)^n] - 1*(1+i)^{-n}]\} = i/\{1 - (1+i)^{-n}]\} = 1/pn_{\rceil}i.$

So, we can write:

$i/[(1+i)^n - 1] + i = i/[1 - (1+i)^{-n}].$

With these formulas we can find out the amount of the periodic payment involved in an annuity having in possession the amount of the amount (A) or the present value (P).

For example, if a savings account pays interest of 2.4% per annum compounded monthly, what monthly payment should the customer make in order to obtain an amount of $706.34 after 10 months?

When dividing 2.4% by the 12 months of the year, we have 0.2% of monthly rate.

Then we do:

$R = A*i/[(1+i)^n - 1]$

$R = 706.34*0.002/[(1.002)^{10} - 1]$

$R \approx 706.34*0.002/(1.02018096 - 1) =$

$= 706.34*0.002/0.02018096 =$

$= 1.41268/0.02018096 \approx 70.00063.$

The monthly deposit that the customer must make is therefore R = $70.

(Note: The student should note that the formulas of payment R, depending on the current value P or the future value A, are merely rearranging of the formulas of P and A; so that it is enough to memorize these two formulas and know how to manipulate them to bring the R value to the first member of the equality.)

Exercise **P4.01**

The customer deposits monthly in an account that pays monthly interest **i** a constant amount that after 11 months results in present value P. Obtain the amount of the periodic payment in the cases below.

A) i = 0.4% p.m., P = 537.03.

Resolution:

$R = P*i/[1 - (1+i)^{-n}]$

$R = 537.03*0.004/[1 - 1.004^{-11}] \approx$

$\approx 537.03*0.004/[1 - 0.9570379] =$

$= 537.03*0.004/0.0429621 = 2.14812/0.0429621 \approx 50.00035.$

Answer: The periodic payment is R = $50.

B) i = 0.5% p.m., A = 1067.71. C) i = 0.4% p.m., A = 859.25. D) i = 0.3% p.m., A = 1296.55. E) i = 0.3% p.m.,

A = 2160.91.

Exercise **P4.02**

Ulysses deposited for 13 months at monthly interest **i** a certain periodic payment. While having obtained amount A, find out what the periodic payment was.

A) i = 0.3% p.m., A = 1191.30.

Resolution:

$R = A*i/[(1+i)^n - 1]$

$R = 1191.30*0.003/[(1.003)^{13} - 1] \approx$

$\approx 1191.30*0.003/[1.0397098 - 1] = 1191.30*0.003/0.0397098 =$

$= 3.5739/0.0397098 \approx 90.00045.$

Answer: The periodic payment is R = $90.

B) i = 0.4% p.m., A = 1331.67. C) i = 0.5% p.m., A = 2411.51. D) i = 0.3% p.m., A = 3970.98. E) i = 0.2% p.m., A = 1842.00.

Exercise **P4.03**

We were using the multiplier amount, $1/an\rceil i$, to get the periodic payment amount. While assuming that the law now requires us to use the present value multiplier for this purpose, find that multiplier in the cases below.

A) $1/an\rceil i = 0.0948$, i = 0.4% p.m.

{Note.: Realize that, instead of $R = A*1/an\rceil i$, we will have $R = P*(1/pn\rceil i + i)$, i. e., instead of $R = A*i/[(1+i)^n - 1]$, we will have $R = P*i/[1 - (1+i)^{-n}].$}

Resolution:

$1/pn\rceil i = 1/an\rceil i + i$

$1/pn\rceil i = 0.0948 + 0.004$

$1/pn\rceil i = 0.0988.$

B) $1/an\rceil i = 0.0948$, i = 0.25% p.m. C) $1/an\rceil i = 0.0856$, i = 0.3% p.m. D) $1/an\rceil i = 0.0911$, i = 0.5% p.m. E) $1/an\rceil i = 0.0992$, i = 0.35% p.m.

Deadline

As we saw earlier, to obtain **n**, the payment term, from the other data, we need to use the logarithms.

With the amount formula, we have:

$A = R[(1+i)^n - 1]/i \Leftrightarrow Ai/R = [(1+i)^m - 1] \Leftrightarrow 1 + Ai/R = (1+i)^n.$

When applying logarithms to both members of the equality, we will have:

$\log(1 + Mi/R) = \log[(1+i)^n] \Leftrightarrow \log(1 + Mi/R) = n{*}\log(1+i).$

Thus:

$$n = \frac{[\log(1 + Ai/R)]}{[\log(1+i)]}$$

Or, writing on the same line, $n = \log(1 + Ai/R)/\log(1+i)$.

In analogous work with the present value formula, we are left with:

$P = R[1 - (1+i)^{-n}]/i \Leftrightarrow Pi/R = 1 - (1+i)^{-n} \Leftrightarrow 1 - Pi/R = (1+i)^{-n}.$

The application of decimal logarithms to both members of the equality gives us:

$\log(1 - Pi/R) = \log[(1+i)^{-n}]$

$\log(1 - Pi/R) = -n{*}\log(1+i)$

$n = -\log(1 - Pi/R)/\log(1+i)$

$n = \log[(1 - Pi/R)^{-1}]/\log(1+i)$

$n = \log[1/(1 - Pi/R)]/\log(1+i)$

$n = \log\{1/[(R - Pi)/R]\}/\log(1+i)$

Finally

$$n = \frac{[\log(R/(R - Pi))]}{[\log(1+i)]}$$

Or, in one line: $n = \log[R/(R - Pi)]/\log(1+i)$

As an example, let us get the number of months required for a periodic payment of $90 at 0.5% monthly interest to yield an amount A = $1200.

We have: A = $1200, R = $90, i = 0.005.

$n = \log(1 + Ai/R)/\log(1+i)$

$n = \log(1 + 1200*0.005/90)/\log(1.005)$

$n \approx \log(1 + 0.06667)/\log(1.005)$

$n = \log(1.06667)/\log(1.005)$

$n \approx 0.02803/0.00217$

$n \approx 12.91705$

The number of months must therefore be n = 13.

Annuity interest

Unlike the cases of amount, present value and deadline, a simple formula for interest on annuities is not obtained. As the current calculators are equipped with a function that allows to obtain roots of polynomial equations, we can find the interest rate through an equation of this type.

With the amount formula, we do:

$A = R[(1+i)^n-1]/i \Leftrightarrow Ai/R = (1+i)^n -1 \Leftrightarrow A(1+i-1)/R = (1+i)^n -1 \Leftrightarrow A(1+i)/R - A/R = (1+i)^n -1$.

This results in the equation:

$(1+i)^n - (A/R)(1+i) + A/R-1 =0$.

Making x = 1 + i and Q = A/R, we can write the polynomial squared as:

$$x^n - Qx + Q - 1 = 0.$$

In an analogous work with the present value formula, we do:

$P = R[1 - (1+i)^{-n}]/i \Leftrightarrow Pi/R = 1 - (1+i)^{-n} \Leftrightarrow P(1+i-1)/R = 1 - (1+i)^{-n} \Leftrightarrow P(1+i-1)/R = 1 - (1+i)^{-n} \Leftrightarrow P(1+i)/R - P/R =$

$= 1 - (1+i)^{-n}$.

This results in:

$(1+i)^n + (P/R)(1+i) - P/R - 1 = 0$.

When making $x = 1+i$ and $D = P/R$, we will have:

$x^n + Dx - D - 1 = 0$.

The expression is not yet a polynomial equation, as the variable has a negative exponent.

How to make it a polynomial equation? Since $x = 1 + i$, its value will always be positive (we are not considering the case of negative interest). So let us divide both members of the equality by x.

$x^n + Dx - (D+1) = 0 \Leftrightarrow (1/x)(1/x)^n + D - (1/x)(D+1) = 0$.

This leads to $(1/x)^{n+1} - (D+1)(1/x) + D = 0$.

Our variable is now $1/x$, that is, $1/(1+i)$. When doing $y = 1/x$, we will finally have the polynomial equation below, which can be solved in the calculator:

$$y^{n+1} - (D+1)y + D = 0.$$

Equations like this can be solved manually using the Newton-Raphson Method, which works on the basis of approximations and which is a topic that is beyond the scope of this manual, but which is left as a challenge for research and expansion of knowledge for the student.

Approximate calculation of annuity interest

Without this, and in the absence of a powerful calculator, with the solution of polynomial equations, manuals usually present a method of calculating the interest rate using tables.

Let us take, for example, the case of the citizen who buys a car with a price of $17,300 in cash, but which he pays in installments, with periodic payments of $600, for 32 months. What is the nominal interest rate **i**? And what is the effective rate **j**? [Table data, for p32 ̅i: 28.7311__(2/3)%;

29.1136__(7/12)%, 29.5032__(1/2)% ...]

We have: P = $17.300, R = $600 and n = 32.

We know that $P = R[1 - (1+i)^{-n}]/i$, or $P = R*pn\rceil i$.

So,

$17300 = 600*pn\rceil i \Leftrightarrow pn\rceil i = 17300/600 = 173/6 \approx 28.8333$.

By table data, $p32\rceil i = 28.8333$ is between i = (7/12)% and i = (2/3)%. The effective rate **j** (j = 12*i) is, therefore, between 7% and 8%, composed monthly.

Exercise **P4.04**

Obtain the number of months required for a periodic payment of $100 to produce the indicated income, in each of the cases below.

A) A = $1436.98, i = 0.4% p.m.

Resolution:

$n = \log(1 + Ai/R)/\log(1+i)$

$n = \log(1 + 1436.98*0.004/100)/\log(1+0.004) =$

$= \log(1 + 0.0574792)/\log(1+0.004) \approx \log(1.05748)/\log(1.004)$.

$N \approx 0.02427/0.001734 \approx 13.99654$.

Answer: It is necessary to wait 14 months.

B) A = $1531.90, i = 0.3% p.m. C) A = $1127.90, i = 0.5% p.m. D) A = $1642.68, i = 0.35% p.m. E) A = $1727.46, i = 0.2% p.m.

Exercise **P4.05**

Obtain the number of months required for a periodic payment of $120 at monthly interest **i** to correspond to the indicated present value.

A) P = $1,527.69, i = 0.3% p.m.

Resolution:

We have: P = $1,527.69, i = 0.003, R = $120.

$n = \log[R/(R - Pi)]/\log(1+i)$

$n = \log[120/(120 - 1527.69*0.003)]/\log(1+0.003)$

$n = \log[120/(120 - 4.58307)]/\log(1+0.003)$

$n = \log[120/115.41693]/\log(1+0.003)$

n -= log1.03971/log1.003

n -= 0.01691/0.001301 = 12.99769.

Answer: The number of months is 13.

B) P = \$1.743.67, i = 0.4% p.m. C) P = \$1506.73, i = 0.5% p.m. D) P = \$1863.54, i = 0.35% p.m. E) P = \$1412.30, i = 0.3% p.m.

Exercise P4.06

While using the polynomial equation $x^n - Qx + Q - 1 = 0$, where $x = 1 + i$ and $Q = A/R$, and a periodic payment of \$100, find out the amount in each case below.

A) i = 0.5% p.m, n = 11 months.

Resolution:

$Q = A/R = A/100$.

$x^n - Qx + Q - 1 = 0$.

$(1+0.005)^{11} - (A/100)(1+0.005) + A/100 - 1 = 0$

$1.005^{11} - (A/100)(1.005) + A/100 - 1 = 0$

$1.0563958 - 0.01005A + 0.01M - 1 = 0$

$0.0563958 - 0.00005A = 0$

$0.00005A = 0.0563958$

$A = 0.0563958/0.00005 \approx 1127.92$.

Answer: The amount will be A = \$1127.92.

B) i = 0.4% p.m., n = 12 months. C) i = 0.3% p.m., n = 18 months. D) i = 0.6% p.m., n = 16 months. E) i = 0.5 p.m., n = 20 months.

Exercise P4.07)

Cincinatus bought a used tractor of present value P, paying in periodic monthly installments of value R, for 15 months. Find out the nominal rate **i** and the effective interest rate **j** in the given situations.

A) P = \$1930, R = \$135.

Resolution:

$P = R[1 - (1+i)^{-n}]/i$.

$P = R*pn\rceil i$

$1930 = 135*pn\overline{|}i \Leftrightarrow pn\overline{|}i = 1930/135 \approx 14.2963$.

By the Table of Present Value of the Annuity of **i**, for n = 15 months, $pn\overline{|}i$ is between 14.2293 [(2/3)%] and 14.3225 [(7/12)%].

To obtain **j**, we will multiply these percentages by 12 months.

Answer: **i** between (7/12)% and (2/3)%, **j** between 7% and 8%, composed monthly.

[Table data, with n = 15 months:

14.7042___(1/4)%; 14.6074___(1/3)%; 14.5116___(5/12)%;

14.4166___(1/2)%; 14.3225___(7/12)%; 14.2293___(2/3)%.]

B) P = $2150, R = $150, C) P = $2050, R = $140, D) P = $2323, R = = $160, E) P = $1877, R = $130

Supplementary exercises

S4.01
Elisa made periodic payments for 14 months, at monthly interest i = 0.4%, having obtained the amount A = $1149.60. What is the R value of the periodic payment?

S4.02
With an estimated present value of P = $1649.30, Manuela invested a certain amount for 13 months, at monthly interest i = 0.35%. Find out the value R of that periodic payment.

S4.03
A bank pays interest at 6% per annum compounded semiannually. Citizen X makes a plan for periodic annual deposits worth $600. Find out the value of citizen Y's periodic semiannual payment so that it is equivalent to that of citizen X (note: It is the present value of one and the other that has to match).

S4.04

Obtain the period, in number of months, for a periodic payment of \$105 at 0.3% monthly interest to result in an amount A = \$2150.

S4.05

Severus bought a drone with a cash value (present value) of \$3,780, but he paid in periodic monthly installments of R = \$195, for 20 months. Find out the nominal rate **i** and the effective interest rate **j**. [Table data, for p20⌉i: 19.1511 ___ (5/12)%; 19.3168 ___ (1/3)%, 19.4845 ___ (1/4)% ...]

Chapter 5 – Amortization

The process of writing off a debt and its respective interest is called amortization through periodic payments, made at equal intervals of time.

When the periodic payments are equal, even including interest, the calculations do not differ from those we have studied before, since we have a simple ordinary annuity there.

At any point during the payment process, the part of the debt that has not yet been paid after a given payment is called the *debit balance*, which corresponds to the present value of the debt at that time. At the moment immediately prior to the payment in question, the unpaid part is called the *debt status*.

The complementary part of the debit balance in the total debt, that is, the part that has already been paid, is called the *equity of the payer*. Correspondingly, the *equity of the recipient*, or seller, is exactly equal to the balance due.

Let us take as an example the case of a customer who buys a product by contracting a debt with a present value of $4000, committing to pay during the next six months six equal installments, including interest, which are 0.6% per month. How much is the amount of the installment in the amortization process?

We have:

$P = \$4000$, $n = 6$ months, $i = 0.006$.

$R = P * i / [1 - (1+i)^{-n}]$

$R = 4000 * 0.006 / [1 - 1.006^{-6}] \approx$

$\approx 4000 * 0.006 / [1 - 0.96474407] =$

$= 4000 * 0.006 / [0.03525593] = 24/0.03525593 \approx 680.7365$.

Answer: The value of the installments is $680.74.

Amortization schedule

The *amortization schedule*, or *Price Table*, created in 1711 by English mathematician Richard Price, is a table that exposes, from period to period, the debit balance, the interest due at the time, the amount of the periodic payment and the amortized portion (discounted R interest) in that period. The table also takes the names of *French Amortization System* (FAS), as France was the center for the dissemination of its use, or *Constant Amortization System* (CAS).

Let us make an amortization schedule for the example above.

Amortization schedule

Period	debit balance	interest due	payment	amortized portion
	$(a=a'-d')$	$(b=a*i)$	$(c=R)$	$(d=c-b)$
1	4000	24.00	680.74	656.74
2	3343.26	20.06	680.74	660.68
3	2682.58	16.01	680.74	664.64
4	2017.94	12.11	680.74	668.63
5	1349.31	8.10	680.74	672.64
6	676.67	4.06	680.74	676.68
Total	-0.01	84.43	4084.44	4000.01

Note: The differences in cents in total are the result of rounding that occur over the periods.

To find the debit balance in any period, while using the

present value formula, just take **n** as the number of remaining installments.

So, after the first payment, in the example above, we have:

$n = 6-1 = 5$, $i = 0.6\%$ p.m., $R = 680.74$.

$P = R[1 - (1+i)^{-n}]/i$

$P = 680.74 \ [1 - 1.006^{-5}] / 0.006 \approx$

$\approx 680.74[1 - 0.9705325297]/0.006 =$

$= 680.74[0.0294674703]/0.006 \approx$

$\approx 680.74*4.91124505 \approx 3343.28$

(Again, the differences in cents, compared to the value already found in the table, are due to rounding.)

To find equity, at any point in the series of payments, simply deduct the debit balance from present value P. For that first month, from the example above, just make

$$4000.00 - 3343.28 = 656.72.$$

In the same example, we will find equity after the payment of the fourth installment.

We have:

$n = 6-4 = 2$, $i = 0.6\%$, $R = 680.74$.

$P = R[1 - (1+i)^{-n}]/i$

$P = 680.74[1 - 1.006^{-2}]/0.006 \approx$

$\approx 680.74[1 - 0.98810714]/0.006 \approx$

$\approx 680.74[0.01189286]/0.006 \approx 680.74*1.98214333 \approx$

$\approx 1349.32.$

The equity at that time is $4000.00 - 1349.32 = 2650.68$.

If we change the column of interest in the table above to that of equity, which is the column of the debit balance backwards, we can draw the graph below. (Black columns: debit balance; white columns: equity; gray columns: amortized portion.)

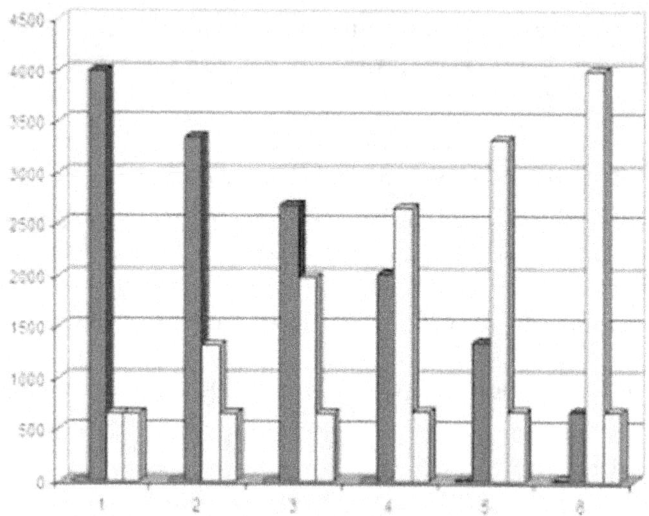

Sinking funds or amortization funds

Sinking funds, or *surrender funds*, are deposits made periodically in an account that aims to pay off a debt of a certain amount (future value). Right after the last deposit, the amount of the account must match the amount of the debt being paid.

The biggest difference between the simple case of repayment and this is that there are now two interest rates: that of the creditor, as before, and that of the fund.

Take, for example, a debt of $6000, to be paid in eight semester periods, at 3% interest compounded semiannually. The amortization fund pays 2% interest compounded every six months. Find out the amount of R, periodic payment, and the amount of the debt service, i. e., R plus the interest of the fund.

We have:

A = $ 6000, i = 3%/2 = 1.5%, n = 8 semesters.

$R = A*i/[(1+i)^n - 1]$

$R = 6000*0.015/[(1 + 0.015)^8 − 1]$

$R = 6000*0.015/[(1.015)^8 - 1] \approx$

$\approx 6000*0.015/[1.12649259 - 1] \approx$

$\approx 6000*0.015/[0.12649259] \approx 6000*0.11858402 \approx$

$\approx 711.504.$

When adjusting the cents for the ceiling (there can be no money at the end), we get R = 711.51.

To calculate the debt service we have to obtain the semiannual interest of the fund, which has a semiannual rate j = 2%/2 = 1%.

We do: 6000*0.01 = 60.

The semiannual debt service will be 711.51+60.00 = 761.51.

Now let us make the table for the amortization fund of the example we just saw.

Amortization fund table

Period	interest	deposit	fund increase	amount of end of period
	(a=d'*i)	(b=R)	(c=a+b)	(d=d'+c)
1	0	711.51	711.51	711.51
2	10,67	711.51	722.18	1433.69
3	21,51	711.51	733.02	2166.71
4	32,5	711.51	744.01	2910.72
5	43,66	711.51	755.17	3665.89
6	54,99	711.51	766.5	4432.39
7	66,49	711.51	778	5210.39
8	78,16	711.51	789.67	6000.06
Total:	307.98	5692.08	6000.06	

d': d of the previous line.

(Note that the interest column total plus the deposit column total gives exactly the fund's increase column.)

How will we find the amount for a given time? Just take the period and apply the amount formula for periodic payments. For example, what will be, in the example above, the amount just after the third payment?

We have:

$R = 711.51$, $i = 3\%/2 = 1.5\%$, $n = 3$.

$A = R[(1+i)^n - 1]/i$.

$A = 711.51[(1.015)^3-1]/0.015 \approx 711.51[1.0456784-1]/0.015 \approx$
$\approx 711.51[0.0456784]/0.015 \approx 711.51*3.0452267 \approx 2166.71$.

Thus, the amount in the third period is $2,166.71, confirming what is in the table.

Exercise P5.01

A customer purchases a product by contracting a debt of present value P, for which he will make periodic payments, including interest of **i** per month, over the next **n** months. Obtain the value of these equal installments in the amortization process, for the cases below.

A) $P = \$8,000$, $n = 10$ months, $i = 0.5\%$ p.m.

Resolution:

$P = \$ 8000$, $n = 10$ months, $i = 0.005$.

$R = P*i/[1 - (1 + i)^{-n}]$

$R = 8000*0.005/[1 - 1.005^{10}] \approx$
$\approx 8000*0.005/[1-0.95134794] =$
$= 8000*0.005/[0.04865206] \approx 8000*0.10277057 \approx$
≈ 822.16456.

The periodic payout will be $822.17 (with a ceiling on cents here).

B) $P = \$7,000$, $n=9$ months, $i = 0.7\%$ p.m. C) $P = \$10,000$, $n = 11$ months, $i = 0.4\%$ p.m. D) $P = \$40,000$, $n = 12$ months, $i = 0,6\%$ p.m. E) $P = \$ 12,000$, $n = 14$ months, $i = 1\%$ p.m.

Exercise **P5.02**
A debt of present value P will be paid in five months (n=5), in equal periodic payments, with monthly interest **i**. Obtain the amount of the periodic payment and build the Price Table.
A) P = $ 7,000, i = 0.4% p.m.
Resolution:
$R = P*i/[1 - (1+i)^{-n}]$
$R = 7000*0.004/[1 - (1.004)^{-5}] \approx$
$\approx 7000*0.004/[1 - 0.98023777779] =$
$= 7000*0.004/[0.01976222221] \approx 7000*0.202406387 \approx$
$\approx 1416.8447.$
The periodic payment is $1,416.84.

Period	debit balance	interest due	payment	amortized portion
	(a=a'-d')	(b=a*i)	(c=R)	(d=c-b)
1	7000	28.00	1416.84	1388.84
2	5611.16	22.44	1416.84	1394.4
3	4216.76	16.87	1416.84	1399.97
4	2816.79	11.27	1416.84	1405.57
5	1411.22	5.64	1416.84	1411.2

(The difference of 2 cents, from a+b to c, is due to rounding.)

B) P = $8,000, i = 0.3% p.m. C) P = $10,000, i = 0.7% p.m. D) P = $6,000, i = 0.8% p.m. E) P = $5,000, i = 0.2% p.m.

Exercise **P5.03**
For the data and results of the previous year, obtain, with the formula, the balance due immediately after the second

payment and the corresponding amount of equity.

A) $P = \$7,000$, $i = 0.4\%$ p.m.

Resolution:

The new **n** will be $n = 5 - 2 = 3$.

$P = R[1 - (1+i)^{-n}]/i$

$P = 1416.84[1 - 1.004^{-3}]/0.004$

$P \approx 1416.84[1 - 0.9880954]/0.004 =$

$\quad = 1416.84[0.0119046]/0.004 =$

$\quad = 1416.84*2.97615 = 4216.728366$.

The debit balance is \$4,216.73.

The equity will be $\$7,000 - \$4,216.73 = \$2,783.27$.

(The difference of 3 cents in the debit balance in relation to the value of the table comes from the difference in rounding.)

B) $P = \$8,000$, $i = 0.3\%$ p.m. C) $P = \$10,000$, $i = 0.7\%$ p.m. D) $P = \$6,000$, $i = 0.8\%$ p.m. E) $P = \$5,000$, $i = 0.2\%$ p.m.

Exercise **P5.04**

Gabrielle made a debt of amount A to be paid over six months (n=6), in equal installments, including interest of $i = 0.4\%$ per month. Obtain the monthly payment amount and the debt service amount, for an amortization fund that pays monthly interest at rate **j**. Build the fund table.

A) $A = \$8000$, $j = 0.3\%$.

$R = A*i/[(1+i)^{n} - 1]$

$R = 8000*0.004/[(1+0.004)^{6} - 1] \approx$

$\quad \approx 8000*0.004/[1.02424128 - 1] =$

$\quad = 8000*0.004/[0.02424128] \approx$

$\quad \approx 8000*0.16500779 = 1320.06$.

The periodic payment is \$1,320.06.

The debt service will be:

$\quad A*j+R = 8000*0.003+1320.06 = 24+1320.06 = 1344.06$.

Amortization fund table

Period	interest	deposit	fund increase	amount of end of period
	(a=d'*i)	(b=R)	(c=a+b)	(d=d1+c)
1	0.00	1320.06	1320.06	1320.06
2	5.28	1320.06	1325.24	2645.3
3	10.58	1320.06	1330.64	3975.94
4	15.90	1320.06	1335.96	5311.9
5	21.25	1320.06	1341.31	6653.21
6	26.61	1320.06	1346.67	7999.88
Total:	79.62	7920.36	7999.88	

B) A =$10000, j = 0.25%. C) A =$5000, j = 0.45%. D) A =$6000, j = 0.3%. E) A =$9500, j = 0.2%.

Depreciation

When someone buys a new car, he knows that the reduction in value of the item compared to the original cost is greater in the early times than in subsequent times. This fall in value is the depreciation of the product. Although there is a simplified method for calculating this drop, while considering it to be linear, the most sensible choice is to use the fixed percentage method, which allows to represent the decrease of the value according to the appropriate curve, which is that of a decreasing exponential function.

In general we consider that our product, almost always a machine, bought at an *original cost* C, has a *useful life* in perfectly functional condition of **n** years, reaching at the end of that period a *residual value*, or *salvage value*, which we denote by S.

To find the depreciation amount per period, Dp, in the linear method, just make the difference C - S and divide by **n**.

For example, if a machine cost $10,000 and has a useful life of 8 years, when it will have a residual value of $1000, then the depreciation per year will be:

$Dp = (C-S)/n$

$Dp = (10,000 - 1000)/8 = 9000/8 = 1,125.$

That amount of $1125 will be deducted each year from the original cost, until the residual value is reached, in the eighth year.

By applying the fixed percentage method, or the constant rate, we can build a depreciation table more in line with the real world. In the first year, depreciation will reduce the original cost value in C*i, so that the product will be worth C - C*i, or C(1-i). In the second year, the value will be $C(1-i)^2$. At the end of the n-year period, with all the discounts made, we will have the following relationship:

$$S = C(1-i)^n$$

Have we seen this formula? Almost. It is the same as the amount, but with C of original cost instead of C of invested capital and with subtraction 1-i, instead of sum 1+i. Let us calculate the constant rate **i** for the example above.

We have:

$S = C(1-i)^n$

$1000 = 10,000 (1-i)^8$

$(1-i)^8 = 1000/10000$

$(1-i)^8 = 0.1 \Leftrightarrow 1-i = 0.1^{1/8} \Leftrightarrow i = 1 - 0.1^{1/8}.$

$i \approx 1 - 0.7498942 = 0.2501058.$

Thus, the constant rate of depreciation of our machine will be 25.01%.

Let us now build the depreciation table for our machine of $10,000 while using the fixed percentage method.

At the end of year 1, the book value is $C(1-i)$ =

$= 10000(1-0.2501)^1 = 10000*0.7499 = 7499$.

For year 2, the book value is $C(1-i)^2 = 10000*0.7499^2 =$

$= 5623.50$.

We continue this way until the calculation of $C(1-i)^8$.

Depreciation schedule

Year	book valor	depreciation	depreciation amount
	$(a=C(1-i)^n)$	$(b = a'-a)$	$(c = c'+b)$
0	10000	0	0
1	7499	2501	2501
2	5623.5	1875.5	4376.5
3	4217.06	1406.44	5782.94
4	3162.38	1054.68	6837.62
5	2371.47	790.91	7628.53
6	1778.36	593.11	8221.64
7	1333.59	444.77	8666.41
8	1000.06	333.53	8999.94

(Note: Since the calculations were made from the values obtained for the first column, the cents that were missing at the end of column **c** are those that were left at the end of column **a**, because of the intermediate rounding.)

Exercise **P5.05**

A company buys a machine with a cost value C knowing that it will work for six years, after which it will have only a residual value S. Using the fixed percentage (or constant rate) method, obtain the rate, i. e., build the depreciation schedule for the cases below.

A) C = \$8,000, S = \$1,000.
Resolution:
n = 6 years.
$S = C(1-i)^n$
$1000 = 8000(1-i)^6$
$(1-i)^6 = 1000/8000$
$(1-i)^6 = 0.125 \Leftrightarrow 1-i = 0.125^{1/6} \approx 0.70710678.$
$i \approx 1 - 0.70710678 = 0.29289322.$
Thus, i = 29.289%. (Hence, 1-i = 0.70711.)

Depreciation schedule

Year	book valor	depreciation	depreciation amount
	$(a=C(1-i)^n)$	(b = a'-a)	(c = c'+b)
0	8000	0	0
1	5656.88	2343.12	2343.12
2	4000.04	1656.84	3999.96
3	2828.47	1171.53	5171.49
4	2000.04	828.43	5999.92
5	1414.25	585.79	6585.71
6	1000.02	414.23	6999.94

(In the final month, a+c should result in the original cost.)
B) C = \$6,000, S = \$800. C) C = \$9,000, S = \$1,500. D) C = \$11,000, S = \$1,100. E) C = \$10,000, S = \$2,000.

What we saw above was a simple depreciation table, with no investment involved other than the original cost of the machine. It is also customary, in addition to this procedure, to create a depreciation fund, using the amortization fund, for a given interest rate and a periodic payment calculated on the data of the asset that is being depreciated.

Take the case of a milling machine purchased for $20,000, which after six years will have a residual value of $1600. At that time, one invests in a depreciation fund that pays interest of 2% per year. Let us calculate the periodic payment that must be made and set up the
depreciation fund table.

We have:

C = $20,000, S = 2000, i = 0.02, n = 6.

A = 20000 − 1600 = 18400.

$R = A*i/[(1+i)^n − 1]$

$R = 18400*0.02/[(1+0.02)^6 − 1] \approx$

$\approx 18400*0.02/[1.12616242 − 1] =$

$= 18400*0.02/0.12616242 \approx 18400*0.1585258 =$

$= 2{,}916.87472.$

We will therefore have periodic payments in the value of R = $2,916.87.

Depreciation fund table

Year	depreciation amount	interest	fund increase	fund amount	book value
	(a)	(b=d'*i)	(c=a+b)	(d=d'+c)	(e=e'-c)
0	0	0	0	0	20000
1	2916.87	0	2916.87	2916.87	17083.13
2	2916.87	58.34	2975.21	5892.08	14107.92
3	2916.87	117.84	3034.71	8926.79	11073.21
4	2916.87	178.54	3095.41	12022.2	7977.8
5	2916.87	240.44	3157.31	15179.51	4820.49
6	2916.87	303.59	3220.46	18399.97	1600.03

As in the amortization fund table seen earlier, if we want to find out the amount right after a given payment, without resorting to the table, we simply use the annuity amount formula.

So, if, for example, we want to know the amount right after the fourth payment, in the case of our machine of $20,000, we follow the procedure below.

We have:

$R = 2916.87$, $i = 0.02$, $n = 4$.

$A = R[(1+i)^n - 1]/i$.

$A = 2916.87[(1.02)^4 - 1]/0.02 \approx 2916.87[1.0824322 - 1]/0.02 =$
     $= 2916.87[0.0824322]/0.02 = 2916.87 * 412161 =$
     $= 12022.2005607$.

The amount right after the fourth payment is $12,022.20.

Exercise **P5.06**

Julius bought a machine for a value C, which will be deactivated in five years, with a residual value S. A depreciation fund will be created, with interest at rate **i** per annum. Obtain the periodic payment to be made and set up the depreciation fund table.

A) $C = \$12.000$, $S = \$2.000$, $i = 3\%$.

Resolution:

$n = 5$ years.

$A = 12000 - 2000 = 10000$

$R = A*i/[(1+i)^n - 1]$

$R = 10000*0.03/[(1+0.03)^5 - 1] \approx$
     $\approx 10000*0.03/[1.15927407 - 1] =$
     $= 10000*0.03/[0.15927407] \approx 10000*0.188354576 =$
     $= 1883.54576$.

The periodic payment will be R = $1,883.55.

Depreciation fund table

Year	depreciation amount	interest	fund increase	fund amount	book value
	$(a=R)$	$(b=d'*i)$	$(c=a+b)$	$(d=d'+c)$	$(e=e'-c)$
0	0	0	0	0	12000
1	1883.55	0	1883.55	1883.55	10116.45
2	1883.55	56.51	1940.06	3823.61	8176.39
3	1883.55	114.71	1998.26	5821.87	6178.13
4	1883.55	174.66	2058.21	7880.08	4119.95
5	1883.55	236.4	2119.95	10000.03	2000

(In the final period, d+e must coincide with the cost value C.)

B) C = \$10,000, S = \$1,200, i = 2%. C) C = \$11,000, S = \$1,000, i = 4%. D) C = \$18,000, S = \$2,000, i = 2%. E) C = \$30,000, S = \$5,000, i = 2.5%.

Depletion

We call *depletion*, or *exhaustion*, the process of depleting the value of a mine, of iron, oil, coal, copper or other good, during its economic exploitation.

Everything happens as if we have a case of linear depreciation, although it is not a machine or other capital asset.

Take the case of a mine whose net annual operating income is valued at \$210,000, with an estimated useful life of 10 years, at the end of which it will have a residual value of \$100,000. The expected return, in relation to the purchase value C, is 6%. If the deposit in a replacement fund earns interest of 3% per annum, what was the purchase price?

We have:

$S = \$100,000$, $r = 6\% = 0.06$, $R' = \$210,000$, $n=10$, $i = 3\% = 0.03$.

$R = A*i/[(1+i)^n - 1]$

In this situation,

$R' = C*r + (C-S)*i/[(1+i)^n - 1]$

$210,000 = 0.06*C + (C-100,000)*0.03/[(1+0.03)^{10} - 1]$.

So,

$0.06*C + C*0.03/[(1.03)^{10} - 1] =$

$= 210,000 + 100,000*0.03/[(1.03)^{10} - 1]$

$\{0.06 + 0.03/[(1.03)^{10} - 1]\}*C =$

$= 210,000 + 100,000*0.03/[(1.03)^{10} - 1]$

$\{0.06 + 0.03/[1.3439164 - 1]\}*C \approx$

$\approx 210,000 + 100,000*0.03/[1.3439164 - 1]$

$(0.06 + 0.03/0.3439164)*C \approx$

$\approx 210,000 + 100,000*0.03/0.3439164$

$(0.06 + 0.0872305)*C \approx 210,000 + 100,000* 0.0872305$

$0.1472305*C = 210,000 + 8,723,05$

$0.472305*C = 218,723.05$

$C \approx 218,723.05/0.1472305$

$C \approx 1,485,582.471023$

The purchase value was $C \approx \$1,485,582.47$.

Exercise **P5.07**

A mine with a yield rate **r** offers an annual income R' for eight years, at the end of which it will have a salvage value S. The deposit in a replacement fund earns interest at an annual rate **i**. For the values below, what was the purchase price C?

A) $R'=\$150,000$, $S = \$20,000$, $r = 5\%$, $i = 4\%$.

Resolution:

$n = 8$ years.

$R' = C*r + (C-S)*i/[(1+i)^n - 1]$

$150000 = 0.05*C + (C-20000)*0.04/[(1+0.04)^8 - 1]$

$0.05*C + C*0.04/(1.04^8 - 1) =$

$$= 150{,}000 + 20{,}000 * 0.04/[1.04^8 - 1]$$
$$\{0.05 + 0.04/(1.04^8 - 1]\} * C =$$
$$= 150{,}000 + 20{,}000 * 0.04/[1.04^8 - 1]$$
$$\{0.05 + 0.04/(1.36856905 - 1]\} * C =$$
$$= 150{,}000 + 20{,}000 * 0.04/[1.36856905 - 1]$$
$$\{0.05 + 0.10852783\} * C = 150{,}000 + 20{,}000 * 0.10852783$$
$$\{0.05 + 0.10852783\} * C = 150{,}000 + 2{,}170.5566$$
$$0.15852783 * C = 152{,}170.5566$$
$$C = 152{,}170.5566/0.15852783$$
$$C = 959{,}898.060801059.$$

The purchase value was C = \$959,898.06.

B) R'=\$200,000, S = \$40,000, r = 6%, i = 5%. C) R'=\$160,000, S = \$30,000, r = 4%, i = 3%. D) R'=\$250,000, S = \$50,000, r = 6%, i = 3%. E) R'=\$50,000, S = \$10,000, r = 7%, i = 5%.

Annuities in advance

We closed this chapter with the theme of *annuity in advance*, or anticipated annuity, which is more related to the previous chapter than to the present one, but which could cause confusion with the most common situation, of annuity in arrears.

What differentiates the anticipated annuity from the other is that in this case, the first periodic payment is not made at the end of the first period, but at the beginning of it. The well-known case of renting a house that requires one month's advance deposit is one such situation.

The treatment is the same as that already followed in the annuity in arrears, with the difference that we consider the first deposit as a cash payment, and we apply the same procedures as before for the other payments, now as an annuity.

So, if we have an annuity in advance with 12 periodic payments of \$250, for example, we understand the first deposit of \$250 as a cash payment and we use annuity formulas for R = \$250, but with n = 11.

```
|   |   |   |        |    |    |
0   1   2   3   ...   9   10   11
```

If the interest paid is 0.4% p.m., let us calculate the present value V of that annuity.

We have:

R = \$250, n = 11, i = 0.004.

$P = R[1 - (1+i)^{-n}]/i$

$V = R + P$

$V = 250 + 250[1 - 1.004^{-11}]/0.004 \approx$

$\approx 250 + 250[1 - 0.9570379]/0.004 =$

$= 250 + 250[0.0429621]/0.004 \approx$

$\approx 250 + 250*10.740525 \approx$

$\approx 250 + 2685.13125 = 2{,}935.13125$

The present value is $V \approx \$2{,}935.13$.

For the same example, we will calculate the future value F, after the 12th payment.

As interest is levied on all installments, even on that zero installment, which we had considered payment in cash, in the amount we take into account in the formula all payments, also including the interest installment of rate **i** on the amount.

We have:

R = \$250, i = 0.004, n = 12 (**n** is now the total number of payments).

$A = R[(1+i)^n - 1]/i$

$F = (1+i)A$

$F = (1+i)R[(1+i)^n - 1]/i$

$F = 1.004*250[1.004^{12} - 1]/0.004 \approx$

$\approx 1.004*250[1.0490702 - 1]/0.004 \approx$

$\approx 1.004*250[0.0490702]/0.004 \approx$

$\approx 1.004*250*12.26755 = 250*12.3166202 = 3{,}079.15505$
The future value is F = \$3,079.16.

The custom is to use a simpler formula for future value. It is easy to prove that:

$(1+i)\overline{an}|i = a(n+1)|i - 1$

We make:
$(1+i)[(1+i)^n - 1]/i =$
$= [(1+i)(1+i)^n - (1+i)]/i$
$= [(1+i)(1+i)^n - 1 - i]/i$
$= [(1+i)^{n+1} - 1]/i - i/i$
$= [(1+i)^{n+1} - 1]/i - 1$

We will recalculate the future value using this last formula.
$R = \$250, i = 0.004, n = 12$
$F = R[a(n+1)|i - 1]$
$F = R\{[(1+i)^{n+'} - 1]/i - 1\}$
$F = 250[(1.004^{13} - 1)/0.004 - 1] \approx$
$\qquad \approx 250[(1.05326649 - 1)/0.004 - 1]$
$\qquad = 250[0.05326649 /0.004 - 1]$
$\qquad = 250[13.3166225 - 1]$
$\qquad = 250*12.3166225 = 3079.155625.$
The future value is F = \$3,079.16.

Exercise **P5.08**
An annuity in advance with **n** installments is made with periodic payments of \$100 per month, with monthly interest **i**. Obtain the present value V and the future value F for the cases below.
A) n = 10, i = 0.3%.
Resolution:
R = \$100, n = 10.
Present value:
V = R + P

$V = R + R[1 - (1+i)^{-n+1}]/i$

$V = 100 + 100[1 - 1.003^{-9}]/0.003 \approx$

$\approx 100 + 100[1 - 0.97340058]/0.003 \approx$

$\approx 100 + 100[0.02659942]/0.003 \approx$

$\approx 100 + 100*8.86647333 \approx$

$\approx 100 + 886.647333 = 986.647333.$

Future value:

$F = R[a(n+1)'i - 1]$

$F = R\{[(1+i)^{N+1} - 1]/i - 1\}$

$F = 100[(1.003^{11} - 1)/0.003 - 1] \approx$

$\approx 100[(1.03349948 - 1)/0.003 - 1] \approx$

$\approx 100[(0.03349948)/0.003 - 1] \approx$

$\approx 100[11.16649333 - 1] \approx$

$\approx 100[10.16649333] = 1016.649333.$

The present value is V = \$986.65.

The future value is F = \$1,016.65.

B) n = 8, i = 0.4%. C) n = 11, i = 0.2%. D) n = 13, i = 0.5%. E) n = 9, i = 0.6%.

Deferred annuities

A deferred annuity is one whose first payment is made at a later date than that which would be the end of the first capitalization period. An example of this is the case when someone makes a contract to deposit equal monthly payments from the end of January, until the end of March of the following year, but only starts depositing that amount four months later, that is, at the end of May.

Suppose that the monthly amount deposited by the citizen of the example is R = \$160, and that the monthly interest is i = 0.3%. Let us calculate the present value of this annuity. We have:

R = \$160, i = 0.003, n = 15 months, n_o = 4 months (delay). Disregarding the delay period, the present value would be:

$P = R[1 - (1+i)^{-n}]/i$

$P = 160[1 - 1.003^{-15}]/0.003 \approx$

$\approx 160[1 - 0.95606189]/0.003 =$

$= 160[0.04393811]/0.003 \approx 160*14.6460367 =$

$= 2343.365872.$

We will now discount the accumulated delay period.

$P' = R[1 - (1+i)^{-no}]/i$

$P' = 160[1 - 1.003^{-4}]/0.003 \approx$

$\approx 160[1 - 0.9880895]/0.003 =$

$= 160[0.0119105[/0.003 \approx 160*3.97016667 =$

$= 635.2266672.$

The present value will be $V = P - P' =$

$= 2343.365872 - 635.2266672 = 1708.1392048.$

So, $V \approx \$1,708.14$.

To calculate the amount, there is no secret, since the interest income will occur after those months of delay. In the example above, just take n'= 15 - 4. Let us calculate that amount.

We have:

$R = \$160$, $i = 0.003$, $n' = 11$ months.

$A = R[(1+i)^{n'} - 1]/i$

$A = 160[(1+0.003)^{11} - 1]/0.003$

$= 160[1.003^{11} - 1]/0.003 \approx$

$\approx 160[1.0334995 - 1]/0.003 \approx$

$\approx 160[0.0334995]/0.003 =$

$= 160*11.1665 = 1786.64.$

The amount will be $\$1,786.64$.

Exercise **P5.09**

Antoinette made an annuity contract committing to deposit the amount R monthly, for **n** months, under monthly interest **i**, but only managed to start the deposits three months later. Obtain the present value V and the future value A for the data below.

    A) $R = \$120$, $n = 14$ months, $i = 0.4\%$ per month.

Resolution:

$n_o = 3$ months.

Present value:

$P = R[1 - (1+i)^{-n}]/i$

$P = 120[1 - 1.004^{-14}]/0.004 \approx$

   $\approx 120[1 - 0.94564476]/0.004$

   $= 120[0.05435524]/0.004$

   $= 120*13.58881 = 1630.6572.$

$P' = R[1 - (1+i)^{-n_o}]/i$

$P' = 120[1 - 1.004^{-3}]/0.004 \approx$

   $\approx 120[1 - 0.98809536]/0.004$

   $= 120[0.01190464]/0.004 \approx$

   $\approx 120*2.97616 = 357.1392.$

$V = P - P' = 1630.6572 - 357.1392 = 1273.518.$

The present value is $V = \$1{,}273.52$.

Future value:

$R = \$120$, $i = 0.004$, $n' = 14 - 3$ months $= 11$ months.

$A = R[(1+i)^{n'} - 1]/i$

$A = 120[(1+0.004)^{11} - 1]/0.004$

   $= 120[1.004^{11} - 1]/0.004 \approx$

   $\approx 120[1.04489064 - 1]/0.004 =$

   $= 120[0.04489064]/0.004 \approx$

   $\approx 120*11.22266 = 1346.7192.$

The future value is $A = \$1{,}346.72$.

    B) $R = \$200$, $n = 18$ months, $i = 0.2\%$ per month. C) $R = \$110$, $n = 16$ months, $i = 0.3\%$ per month. D) $R = \$220$, $n = 12$ months, $i = 0.4\%$ per month. E) $R = \$300$, $n = 13$ months, $i = 0.5\%$ per month.

Perpetuities

Any annuity with a start date for payments, but no end

date, is assumed to be perpetuity, assuming indefinite validity.

If we understand, against the nature of corporate entities, that a given joint stock company will never be closed, due to bankruptcy or a sovereign decision of its board, then the possession of a lot of its shares generates endless dividend gains, constituting a perpetuity. Another case is the right to a lifetime pension that passes from father to son from generation to generation. In cases of perpetuity it is not possible to obtain the value of a final amount, which simply does not exist.

The value R, periodic payment, is the interest yield, P*i, that the current value P provides in the period in question.

$$R = P*i$$

For example, to find the current value of a share that at the end of each year yields to the holder the amount R = $1.50, with annual interest of 4%, we do:

R = P*i

1.50 = A*0.04

A = 1.50/0.004 = 375.

The share value is $375.

Exercise **P5.10**

Romulus bought a lot of shares that earns him R annually, with annual interest **i**. Obtain the current value of the lot in the given cases.

A) R = $12.60, i = 5%.

Resolution:

R = P*i

12.60 = P*0.05

P = 12.60/0.05 = 252.

The current value of the lot is P = $252.00.

B) R = $10.00, i = 6%. C) R = $15.50, i = 4%. D) R = $20.00, i = 7%. E) R = $9.40, i = 3%.

Capitalized cost

If a given initial cost asset B depreciates in a given period and needs replacements, in a perpetuity of present value P, the capitalized cost of that asset is the value

$$C = B + P$$

Take the case of a machine with initial cost of \$23,000, which must be replaced after 10 years, when it will have a saved value of \$3000. Since \$23,000 is the cost of replacements, at an annual interest rate of r = 5%, let us calculate the capitalized cost of the machine.

The periodic payment to the replacement fund is R =
= B - S = 23000 - 3000 = 20,000.

As R = P*i, we can write P = R/i.

We must obtain interest rate **i**, for the entire 10-year period of depreciation.

We do:

$(1+i)^1 = (1+r)^{10}$

$1+i = 1.05^{10}$

$i = -1 + 1.05^{10} \approx -1 + 1.6288946 = 0.6288946.$

So:

C = B + P (or C = B + R/i)

C = 23000 + 20000/0.6288946 =

= 23000 + 31801.8313403 = 54801.8313403.

The capitalized cost will be C =\$54,801.83.

Exercise **P5.11**

An industrialist buys machines with initial cost B, which work for **n** years, falling to a residual value S. Since B is the cost of replacements, which has an annual interest rate **r**, discover the capitalized cost of each machine in the situations below.

A) B = \$40,000, S = \$5,000, n = 8 years, r = 4%.
We have:
R = 40000 − 5000 = 35000.
$(1+i)^1 = (1+r)^8$
$1+i = 1.04^8$
i = -1 + 1.36856905 = 0.36856905.
C = B + P, i. e., C = B + R/i
C = 40000 + 35000/0.36856905
C = 40000 + 94961.85
C = \$134,964.85.
  B) B = \$30,000, S = \$4,000, n = 9 years, r = 3%. C) B = \$60,000, S = \$2,000, n = 10 years, r = 5%. D) B = \$100,000, S = \$8,000, n = 12 years, r = 4%. E) B = = \$90,000, S = \$8,000, n = 11 years, r = 4.5%.

Supplementary exercises

S5.01
A machine of present value P = \$11,000 is purchased through a debt to be paid with 20 equal periodic payments, at interest of 0.4% per month. Determine the amount of periodic payments.

S5.02
A refrigerator of present value P = \$2,500 was purchased under an equal payments contract for six months, at interest of 0.5% per month. Obtain the installment amount and build the Price Table.

S5.03
A small business owner bought a grinder for \$7,000, for equal payments over five months, at 0.45% interest per month. Determine the monthly payment amount and build the amortization fund table, which pays interest at rate j = 0.4% per month.

S5.04 (see ex P5.05)

Honorius bought a machine at a cost value of C = $9,000, providing for a five-year durability, with a residual value of S = $1,000 for scrap. Using the constant rate method, obtain the interest rate **i** and set up the depreciation table.

S5.05   (see ex P5.06)

An industrialist purchased a machine with a cost value of C = $20,000, to be decommissioned in six years, with a residual value of S = $3,000. At the same time, a depreciation fund was created, with annual interest i = 4%. Determine the amount of the periodic payment and set up the depreciation fund table.

S5.06

Catherine contracted an advance payment of eight installments, for periodic payments of $140 per month, at monthly interest of 0.4%. Calculate the present value and the future value of that annuity.

S5.07

Marina makes monthly advance payments of $250 for 14 months, at 0.3% monthly interest. Jonah, her husband, wants to make monthly payments for the same term, at the same interest rate, but in a postponed manner. Find out the amount of Jonah's monthly payment so that the amount of both is the same.

S5.08

A citizen entered into an annuity contract providing to deposit the monthly amount of $200, for 15 months, at interest of 0.25% per month. The first deposit, however, he only managed to make after four months. Obtain the present value and the future value of this deferred annuity.

S5.09

An investor owns a stock in a company that brings him an annual gain of \$11.50, with interest of i = 3%. Find out the present value of the action.

S5.10

John uses in his factory a machine with initial cost B = = \$25,000, which is deactivated after 10 years, when he retains a residual value of only \$2,500. The cost of replacements is also \$25,000, at an interest rate of r = 3%. Determine the capitalized cost of this machine.

Chapter 6 – Bonds

A *bond*, or *obligation*, is a contract that we sign with a commitment to make periodic payments, at a given interest rate, until a specified future date, called the *surrender date*.

A bond signed with the government is usually called a *bill* or *policy*, while an bond with a private company usually takes the form of a debenture.

On the surrender date, an obligation has a *nominal value*, or *face value*, and a *surrender value*. When these two values coincide, we say that the bond is *redeemable at par*, or redeemable at 100, meaning that the surrender value is 100% of the nominal value (the "%" symbol is usually omitted). If, for example, the face value is \$1000 and the surrender value is \$1200, we say that the bond is redeemable at 120, that is, 120% of the face value, which in this case leads to 1.20*1000.

The purchase price C of a bond on the surrender date, with F being the face value, V the redemption value, **r** the bond's interest rate, **i** the investor's interest rate and **n** the number of periods, is given by formula:

$$C = V*(1+i)^{-n} + Fr*pn{*}i$$

The formula, with two installments, brings the sum of the present value of the surrender value and the present value of the periodic payments.

It is easy to demonstrate the equivalence between the above formula and a simpler one, more frequently used, given by:

$$C = V + (Fr - Vi)pn{*}i$$

For example, be it a \$5,000 par value bond, at 3% p.a. interest, redeemable at 102, within four years, at 5% investor interest, compounded semiannually. What will be its purchase price on the surrender date?

We have:

$F = \$5000$, $V = \$5000 * 1.02 = 5100$, $r = 3\%/2 = 1.5\%$, $i = 5\%/2 = 2.5\%$, $n = 8$ semesters.

$C = V + (Fr - Vi)pn*i$

$C = V + (Fr - Vi)[1 - (1+i)^{-n}]/i$

$C = 5100 + (5000*0.015 - 5100*0.025)[1 - 1.025^{-8}]/0.025$

$C \approx 5100 + (75 - 127.50)[1 - 0.82074657]/0.025 \approx$

$\approx 5100 - 52.50*0.17925343/0.025 \approx$

$\approx 5100 - 52.50*7.1701372 \approx$

$\approx 5100 - 376.432203 = 4723.567797.$

The purchase value is $C = \$4{,}723.57$.

One way to clearly understand the operation of a bond is to prepare an investment table, in which we explain the evolution of the book value, which starts with the purchase value and ends with the surrender value.

For example, let us take an obligation of nominal value $F = \$1{,}000$, at interest of 6% p.a, redeemable at 102, within six semesters, at investor interest of 5%, compounded semiannually.

We have:

$F = 1000$, $V = 1000*1.02 = 1020$, $n = 6$ semesters, $r = 3\%$, $= 2.5\%$.

$C = V + (Fr - Vi)[1 - (1+i)^{-n}]/i$

$C = 1020 + (1000*0.03 - 1020*0.025[1 - 1.025^{-6}]/0.025 \approx$

$\approx 1020 + (30 - 25.50)[1 - 0.86229687]/0.025 \approx$

$\approx 1020 + 4.50[0.13770313]/0.025 \approx$

$\approx 1020 + 4.50*5.5081252 \approx$

$\approx 1020 + 24.7865634 = 1044.7865634.$

The purchase value is $C = \$1{,}044.79$.

Bond investment table

Period	book value	Interest on book value	Interest of bond	Variation of book value
	(a=a'-d')	(b=a*i)	(c=F*r)	(d=c-b)
1	1044.79	26.12	30	3.88
2	1040.91	26.02	30	3.98
3	1036.93	25.92	30	4.08
4	1032.85	25.82	30	4.18
5	1028.67	25.72	30	4.28
6	1024.39	25.61	30	4.39
7	1020			

Now let us assume that in the same 6 semesters we have a bond of $1,000, at 5%, redeemable at 104, with investor interest of 6%, compounded semiannually. Let us make the investment table.

We have:

F = 1000, V = 1000*1.04 = 1040, n = 6 semesters, r = = 2.5%, i = 3%.

$C = V + (Fr - Vi)[1 - (1+i)^{-n}]/i$

$C = 1040 + (1000*0.025 - 1040*0.03[1 - 1.03^{-6}]/0.03 \approx$

$\approx 1040 + (25 - 31.20)[1 - 0.8374843]/0.03 \approx$

$\approx 1040 - 6.20[0.1625157]/0.03 \approx$

$\approx 1040 - 6.20*5.41719 \approx$

$\approx 1040 - 33.586578 \approx 1006.41.$

The purchase price is C = $1,006.41.

Bond investment table

Period	book value	Interest on book value	Interest of bond	Variation of book value
	(a=a'-d')	(b=a*i)	(c=F*r)	(d=c-b)
1	1006.41	30.19	25	-5.19
2	1011.59	30.35	25	-5.35
3	1016.94	30.51	25	-5.51
4	1022.45	30.67	25	-5.67
5	1028.12	30.84	25	-5.84
6	1033.96	31.02	25	-6.02
7	1039.98			

(The difference of 2 cent was due to rounding.)

Exercise **P6.01**

A bond with a nominal value of \$10,000, at annual interest **r** of 4% p.a., is redeemable at 103, within **n** semesters, at annual interest **i** of the investor, compounded semiannually. Obtain the purchase price in the cases below.

A) n = 18 semesters, i = 5% p.a.

Resolution:

We have:

r = 4%/2 = 2%, i = 5%/2 = 2.5%, F = \$10,000, V = = \$10,000*1.03 = \$10,300, n = 18.

$C = V + (Fr - Vi)[1 - (1+i)^{-n}]/i$

$C = 10300 + (10000*0.02 - 10300*0.025)[1 - 1.025^{-18}]/0.025 \approx$

$\approx 10300 + (200 - 257.50)[1 - 0.6411659]/0.025 =$

$= 10300 - 75.50[0.3588341]/0.025 =$

$= 10300 - 75.50*14.353364 =$

$= 10300 - 1083.678982 = 9216.321018.$

The purchase value is C = \$9,216.32.

B) n = 21 semesters, i = 4.4% p.a. C) n = 14 semesters, i = = 2% p.a. D) n = 20 semesters, i = 3% p.a. E) n = 24 semesters, i = 4% p.a.

Exercise **P6.02**

A bond of nominal value F, with annual interest **r** of 5% p.a., is redeemable at 104, within **n** years, at annual interest **i** of the investor. Obtain the face value and the surrender value from its purchase value C, in the cases below.

A) C = \$10,600, n = 10 years, i = 4% p.a.

Resolution:

We have:

r = 6%, i = 4%, V = F*1.04, n = 10, C = \$10,600.

$C = V + (Fr - Vi)[1 - (1+i)^{-n}]/i$

$10600 = F*1.04 + (F*0.05 - F*1.04*0.04)[1 - 1.04^{-10}]/0.04$

$10600 \approx F*1.04 + F(0.05 - 0.0416)[1 - 0.67556417]/0.04$

$10600 = F*1.04 + F(0.0084)[0.32443583]/0.04$

$10600 = F*1.04 + F(0.0084)*8.11089575$

$10600 = F*1.04 + F*0.0681315243$

$10600 \approx F*1.1081315$

$F \approx 10600/1.1081315$

$F \approx 9565.65172996$

$V = F*1.04 = 1.04*9565.65172996 \approx 9948.27779916$

The face value is F = \$9,565.65.

The surrender value is V = \$9,948.28.

B) C = \$10,000, n = 12 years, i = 3.5% p.a. C) C = \$12,000, n = 10 years, i = 3% p.a. D) C = \$11,200, n = 14 years, i = 5% p.a. E) C = \$13,400, n = 11 years, i = 2% p.a.

Annuity bond

An annuity bond is an obligation whose current value, at a given interest rate, coincides with the nominal value F.

Take the case of a 12-year annuity with a nominal value F = = \$18,000 and interest of 5% compounded semiannually, the first payment being made at the end of the first semiannual period. What will be the purchase price C after 17 semesters to have an interest yield of 4%?

As there are 24 semesters, the buyer of the bond will still have $n' = 24 - 17$ years of payments.

We have:

$F = \$18{,}000$, $r = 0.05/2$, $n = 24$, $n' = 7$, $i = 0.04/2$.

$F = R*pn\rceil r$, or $F = R[1 - (1+r)^{-n}]/r$.

$R = F*r/[1 - (1+r)^{-n}]$

$R = 18000*0.025/[1 - 1.025^{-24}] \approx$

$\approx 18000*0.025/[1 - 0.55287535] =$

$= 18000*0.025/[0.44712465] \approx$

$\approx 18000*0.05591282 = 1006.43076.$

The periodic payment is $R = \$1{,}006.43$.

$C = Rpn'\rceil i$

$C = R[1 - (1+i)^{-n'}]/i$

$C = 1006.43[1 - 1.02^{-7}]/0.02 \approx$

$\approx 1006.43[1 - 0.87056018]/0.02 =$

$= 1006.43[0.12943982]/0.02 \approx$

$\approx 1006.43*6.471991 = 6513.60590213.$

The purchase price after 17 semesters to yield 4% p.a. is $C = \$6{,}513.61$.

Exercise **P6.03**

A n-year annuity bond, with a face value of \$50,000 and first payment at the end of the first quarter, at interest $r = 6\%$ compounded quarterly, is sold after n_o years to earn interest **i**, compounded quarterly. Find out the purchase price.

A) $r = 6\%$ per year, $n = 8$ years, $n_o = 2.5$ years, $i = 4\%$ per year.

Resolution:

$F = \$50{,}000$, $r = 0.06/4 = 0.015$, $n = 32$ quarters, $n' = 32 -$

10 quarters, $i = 0.04/4 = 0.01$.

$R = F*r/[1 - (1+r)^{-n}]$

$R = 50000*0.015/[1 - 1.015^{-32}] \approx$

$\approx 50000*0.015/[1 - 0.62099292] =$

$= 50000*0.015/[0.37900708] \approx$

$\approx 50000*0.039577097 = 1978.85485$.

The periodic payment is $R = \$1,978,85$.

$C = R[1 - (1+i)^{-n'}]/i$

$C = 1978.85[1 - 1.01^{-32}]/0.01 \approx$

$\approx 1978.85[1 - 0.80339621]/0.01 =$

$= 1978.85[0.19660379]/0.01 \approx$

$\approx 1978.85*19.660379 \approx 38904.94098$.

The purchase price under the given conditions is $C = \$38,904.94$.

B) $r = 8\%$ per year, $n = 10$ years, $n_o = 3$ years, $i = 6\%$ per year. C) $r = 6\%$ per year, $n = 12$ years, $n_o = 4$ years, $i = 4.8\%$ per year. D) $r = 6\%$ per year, $n = 11$ years, $n_o = 3.5$ years, $i = 3.2\%$ per year. E) $r = 8\%$ per year, $n = 7.5$ years, $n_o = 4$ years, $i = 6\%$ per year.

Supplementary exercises

S6.01
A bond has a nominal value $F = \$4,000$, redeemable at par over 12 years, with interest payments of 6% compounded semiannually. Determine the purchase price C so that it pays interest at 5% compounded semiannually.

S6.02
For a bond of nominal value $F = \$8,000$, redeemable at 106 in 9 years, with 6% compound interest paid semiannually, obtain the purchase value so that it produces interest at 4% compound semiannually.

S6.03

A bond of nominal value F = $5,000, redeemable at 108 in 14 years, with interest of 5.5% per year, must be sold to produce interest of 6% per year. Determine the purchase price.

S6.04

A bond with a face value of F = $8,200, redeemable at par in 18 semesters, with interest of 7% per year compounded semiannually, is sold to produce interest of 6%, compounded semiannually. Determine the purchase price.

S6.05

An annuity bond with face value of $20,000, at 18 years and interest of 5% per year, is purchased after 12 years to earn interest of 4%. Find the purchase price.

S6.06

A 10-year annuity bond, with a par value of $ 28,000 and first payment at the end of the first semester, at 5% interest compounded semiannually, is sold after 6 years in order to produce interest of 3%, compounded semiannually. Obtain the purchase price C under these conditions.

APPENDIX

A) Annuities in Excel

I. Formula of the periodic payment

= PMT(rate, nper, pv, fv, type)

The meanings are:
rate: interest rate applied to the annuity;
nper: total number of payments (periods) of the annuity;
pv: present value of the annuity, or principal;
fv: future value, or amount to be reached;
type: payment time.
Remarks: (a) if the annuity is 16 years, for example, and the interest rate is 4%, compounded semiannually, then nper is taken as 32 (=2*16) and rate as 2% (=4%/2); (b) the value of pv - or that of fv, alternatively - is entered with multiplication by -1; (c) if fv is not filled in, it is understood that it is worth 0 (zero), for example, as the final value of a discount phase; (d) the type is 0 (zero) - or omitted - for postpaid, and 1 for prepaid; (e) every formula of function in Excel starts in the cell with the equality symbol.
Example: For a present value of $20,000, with an interest rate of 2% per year, term of 16 years and payments in arrears, we will obtain the payment amount.

=PMT(2%, 16, -20000, ,0)

After pressing the Enter key, we will have as a result the payment R = $1,473.00.
Obviously, in the first argument, we could have written 0.02 instead of 2%.

We could also have stored these three data in cells, to call them later in another cell where the function was typed. For example, we can write 2%, 16, -20000 and 0, in cells A2, A3, A4 and A5, respectively. Then, in cell B6 we write

= PMT(A2, A3, A4, ,A5)

The result will be exactly the same as before.

Tip: modify some of the numbers in the example to see new results.

II. Present value formula

= PV(rate, nper, pmt, fv, type)

Example: To obtain a future value (amount) of $140,000, at monthly interest of 1%, in payments in arrears, for 24 months, we will write:

= PV(1%, 24, ,-140000)

The result will be P = $110,259.26.

Since the payment R was not provided, the "payment" space had to be left blank (before -140000). The type, which was 0 (postpaid), was also omitted, and as it would be the last argument, we did not have to explain its space in the application of the formula.

III. Formula of the future value

= FV(rate, nper, pmt, pv, type)

Example: To know how much we will have by amount (FV) after 24 months at monthly interest of 1%, with postpaid payments, knowing that our investment totals a present value

(PV) of $100,000, we will do:

$$= FV(1\%, 24, ,-100000)$$

The result will be A = $126,973.46.

IV. Formula of rate

$$= RATE(nper, pmt, pv, fv, type, guess)$$

The argument "guess" is the approximate value that the user expects to have as a rate. When the value is omitted, Excel defaults to 10%. In the vast majority of cases, the information does not need to be filled out.

Example: We find the interest rate per month for an investment of present value $120,000 and future value $150,000, in postpaid payments made during 12 months, making:

$$= RATE (12, ,-120000, 150000, 0)$$

The rate obtained will be i = 1%. The student must not forget the blank space in place of the argument "pmt", which was not provided and is not necessary in this specific example.

V. Formula for the number of periods

$$= NPER(rate, pmt, pv, fv, type)$$

Example: For an investment of $15,000, which expects as a result an amount of $20,158.75, at a rate of 3%, in postpaid payments, we will fill in the formula as follows:

$$= NPER(3\%, -15000, 20158.75, 0)$$

The result will be n = 10.

VI. Formula of Interest income

= PPMT(rate, per, nper, pv; fv, type)

Here, we have to inform the position of the period, before giving the number of periods. For example, the fifth month within a period of 14 months.

Example: To find out the interest income of the eighth month, at 3% monthly, in a series of 10-month payments, postpaid, with a present value of $15,000 and an amount of $20,156.75, we will do:

= PPMT(3%, 8, 10, -15000, 20158.75, 0)

The result will be j = $553.44.

VII. Formula of net present value

= NPV(rate, value1, value2, ...)

Several other formulas of Financial Mathematics besides those of annuity are offered by Excel. One of them is an important one, the net present value.

Example: To find the net present value of an investment of $20,000, at an interest rate of 3%, with surrenders of $ 10,000 and $ 12,000, we will do:

= NPV(3%, -20000, 10000, 12000)

The result will be Npv = $990.18 (see exercise P2.20).

VIII. Formula for the internal rate of return

= IRR(values; guess)

Example: For an investment of $100,000, with expected surrenders of $30,000, $30,000 and $50,000, arranged in cells B11 (such as -100,000), B12, B13 and B14, we will obtain the IRR by typing in any other cell:

= IRR(B11:B14)

The result will be r = 4%. The meaning of the argument "guess" is the same as that already shown for the rate function, and is optional.

IX. Formula for modified internal rate of return

= MIRR(values, finance_rate, reinvest_rate)

MIRR, or Modified IRR, calculates the rate of return while taking into account the rate of reinvestment of assets in the market.

Example: For a cash flow with an initial cost of $40,000 and returns of $11,000, $15,000 and $12,000, entered in cells B8, B9, B10 and B11, with a finance rate of 3% and a reinvestment rate of 8%, we will do:

= MTIR(B8:B11, 3%, 8%)

The result will be 0.85%.

X. Formula of depreciation (constant rate)

= BD(cost, salvage, life, period, month)

Example: To obtain the depreciation charge after the fourth year of a machine costing $8,000, residual value $1,000 and a useful life of six years, we will do:

$$= BD(8000, 1000, 6, 4)$$

The result will be b = \$828.36. There is a small difference in cents compared to what was calculated in exercise P5.05, when we obtained b = \$828.43 (line 4), but these variations are expected, due to rounding.

Other depreciation formulas, using methods other than the constant rate, together with some other formulas of Financial Mathematics, are part of the list of Excel resources. To learn about them, the student can click on an empty cell in the spreadsheet and in the program header click on **fx**, next to the sum symbol (or click Insert menu, so Function). When the window appears, just click on Finance, in the Function Category column.

B) Annuities on HP 12C

I. Calculation of periodic payment

Unless the user wants to use the program mode to automate the processes, while creating a formula, the usual way in using the HP 12C calculator is to store the values to obtain the desired result at the end.

To find out the payment with the same data used in the first Excel example above, where we had a present value of \$20,000, with an interest rate of 2% and a 16-year term, we will follow the steps below, clicking the keys and the amounts indicated.

a) **f**, REG
b) 20000, CHS, PV
c) 2, **i**
d) 16, **n**
e) **g**, END, PMT

The result will be R = $1,473.00, as it was also obtained in the Excel formula. We saw that, unlike what happens with Excel, when typing 2 to store in the **i** key, the "%" symbol is already understood. The CHS key means *Change Signal*. The commas, in steps a, b, c, d, and e, are only there to indicate the separation between the actions, and are not typed.

The student can experience, in the same problem, the result for anticipated payment, instead of the postpaid payment, obtained by pressing **g** and END before PMT. For the advance, just change **g**, END, for **g**, BEG (BEG comes from Begin), which is under the key 7. The value will be a little less than the payment in advance, obviously.

If the student wants only one place after the decimal point to appear on the display, he presses **f**, then the number 1. For two places, **f**, then the number 2, and so on.

If he does not have the physical calculator in hand, it is enough to search for "HP 12C emulator download" in the window of an internet search engine.

II. Calculation of present value

Repeating the example made in Excel, let us take the case of an expected amount of $140,000, at monthly interest of 1%, in postpaid payments, for 24 months. We will obtain the present value.

    a) **f**, REG
    b) 140000, CHS, PV
    c) 1, **i**
    d) 24, **n**
    d) **g**, END
    e) PV

The result will be P = $110,259.26, exactly the same as the one found above.

III. Calculation of future value

Here we take the example of an investment with present value of $65,000, with monthly payments of $280, for 60 months, at interest of 10.8% per year compounded monthly. Let us see what the future value will be.
     a) **f**, REG
     b) 10.8, Enter, 12, :, **i**
     c) 65000, CHS, PV
     d) 280, **g**, END, PMT
     e) 60, **n**
     f) FV

The result will be A = $89,124.38.

IV. Calculation of the number of periods

Let us use the example already seen above. For an investment of $15,000, annual interest of 3%, with postpaid payments, and future value of $20,157.75. To obtain the number of years we will do:
     a) **f**, REG
     b) 3, **i**
     c) 15000, CHS, PV
     d) 20158.75, FV
     e) **g**, END
     f) **n**

The result will be n = 10 years.
If the g-END command is omitted there will be no change, once END mode is the default on the machine.

V. Calculation of rate

In this example, we have a financing whose present value is $75,000, paid in 60 months, postpaid, in installments of $1,714.17. To find out the interest rate of the annuity we will do the following:

    a) **f**, REG
    b) 75000, CHS, PV
    c) 1714.17, PMT
    d) 60, **n**
    e) **g**, END
    f) **i**

The result will be r = 1.1%.

VI. Calculation of interest income

In the HP 12C, the process that corresponds to the calculation of the annuity interest income is done using the AMORT key, of Amortization.

Let us take a present value of $20,000, at interest of 1.5% per month, amortized over 14 months, in a postpaid manner. To obtain the payment of interest for the fourth month, we will do:

    a) **f**, REG
    b) **g**, END
    c) 20000, CHS, PV
    d) 14, **n**
    e) 1.5, **i**
    f) PMT
    g) 1, **f**, AMORT
    h) X><Y

Clicking PMT in step f shows the value of the installment

to be paid, which is $1,549.57. In step g we get the interest from installment number 1, while in step h we have the amortization amount of that installment on the display. This interest payment from step g is not yet the amount sought. To obtain the amount referring to installment number 4, we repeat processes g and h three more times. In this third repetition, step g brings the interest payment and step h, the amortization amount.

The result will be j = $240.87.

VII. Calculation of net present value

Take the case of a deposit of $30,000, at 2.1% monthly interest, with withdrawals of $10,000, $ 11,000 and $ 11,000. We calculate the net present value as follows:

a) **f**, REG
b) 30000, CHS, **g**, CFo
c) 10000, **g**, CFj
d) 1, **g**, Nj
e) 11000, g, CFj
f) 2, **g**, Nj
g) 2.1, **i**
h) **f**, NPV

The result will be Npv = $681.59.

It is a cash flow. The investment is introduced with CHS, g and CFo. CFo, blue key, is under the white PV key. Then we introduce withdrawals. The $10,000 value goes to Cfj, blue key under PMT. As it occurs once, we then type 1, g, Nj. Then we enter $11,000, with g and CFj. It occurs twice, so in the next step we do 2, g, Nj. Now we introduce the interest rate, with 2.1, i. Finally, we type f, NPV. The f key activates the yellow symbols. So it is just to click NPV, net present value, on the white PV key.

VIII. Calculation of the internal rate of return

We can find out the internal rate of return (IRR) of the investment from the example above. For this, we do:

    a) **f**, REG
    b) 30000, CHS, **g**, CFo
    c) 10000, **g**, CFj
    d) 1, **g**, Nj
    e) 11000, **g**, CFj
    f) 2, **g**, Nj
    g) **f**, IRR

The result will be 3.25%.

IX. Calculation of MTIR

In the HP 12C the calculation of MTIR is done through a very detailed, but funny, step-by-step. We bring the cash back to present value (PV), according to the promised reinvestment rate and add these numbers together. We discount the initial cost of the investment to find out if we have a positive result and evaluate whether it is worth investing, and then we take that sum of returns to future value, counting the number of periods involved.

Let us to take an investment of $15,000, which provides for returns of $6,000, $7,000 and $5,000, at the end of the first, second and third years.

Let us first calculate the IRR. We do: **f**, REG; 15000, CHS, **g**, CFo; 6000, **g**, CFj; 1, **g**, Nj; 7000, **g**, CFj; 1, **g**, Nj; 5000, **g**, CFj; 1, **g**, Nj; **f**, IRR. The display will show the value 9.99%, or, if we adjust to three places (f, 3), 9.985%.

Let us now obtain the MTIR value, taking into account that the reinvestment rate will be i = 8%, a value given by the market. First, we will bring each return to present value.

a) **f**, REG; 6000, CHS, FV; 1, **n**; 8, **i**; PV. This gives 5.555,56.

b) **f**, REG; 7000, CHS, FV; 2, **n**; 8, **i**; PV. This gives 6.001,37.

c) **f**, REG; 5000, CHS, FV; 3, **n**; 8, **i**; PV. This gives 3.969,16.

The sum of the three present values gives 15,526.16. It is worth making the contract because this is greater than the initial amount invested, $15,000.

We take that sum to a future value, with that rate of 8%.

a) **f**, REG

b) 15526.16; CHS; PV

c) 3, **n**

d) 8, **i**

e) FV

The display will show $19,558.40.

Now just find out what rate applied to the present value of $15,000 leads to the future value of $19,558.40 after three years.

We do: **f**, REG; 15000, CHS, PV; 19558.40, FV; 3, **n**; **i**.

The result will be 9.25%, which is the MTIR value.

X. Calculation of depreciation (constant rate)

In order not to enter the programming mode, let us manually operate the example given above in Excel, for a machine with a cost of $8,000, a useful life of six years and a salvage value of $1,000. We look for the depreciation charge in the fourth year.

As we saw before, $C*(1-r)^n = S$, which results in $1-r = (S/C)^{1/n}$.

Thus, $i = (S/C)^{1/n} = (1000/8000)^{1/6} = (1/8)^{1/6}$.

At HP 12C we do:

143

1, ENTER, 8, :, Enter, 1, ENTER, 6, :, Y^X.

The result on the display is 0.70711 (if we set the display to five decimal places). We note this value.

The depreciation charge in the fourth year will be equal to the difference between the book value of the third year and that of the fourth year.

We do:

8000, ENTER, 0.70711, X

ENTER, 0.70711, X

ENTER, 0.70711, X

At this point the number on the display is the book value for the third year, $ 2,828.47. We noted that value out. When continuing:

ENTER, 0.70711, X

We now have the book value for the fourth year, which is $2,000.04. We do:

CHS, ENTER

2828.47, +

The result on the display is the fourth year depreciation charge, $929.43.

Table of decimal logarithms

x	0	1	2	3	4	5	6	7	8	9
10	00000	00432	00860	01284	01703	02119	02531	02938	03342	03743
11	04139	04532	04922	05308	05690	06070	06446	06819	07188	07555
12	07918	08279	08636	08991	09342	09691	10037	10380	10721	11059
13	11394	11727	12057	12385	12710	13033	13354	13672	13988	14301
14	14613	14922	15229	15534	15836	16137	16435	16732	17026	17319
15	17609	17898	18184	18469	18752	19033	19312	19590	19866	20140
16	20412	20683	20952	21219	21484	21748	22011	22272	22531	22789
17	23045	23300	23553	23805	24055	24304	24551	24797	25042	25285
18	25527	25768	26007	26245	26482	26717	26951	27184	27416	27646
19	27875	28103	28330	28556	28780	29003	29226	29447	29667	29885
20	30103	30320	30535	30750	30963	31175	31387	31597	31806	32015
21	32222	32428	32634	32838	33041	33244	33445	33646	33846	34044
22	34242	34439	34635	34830	35025	35218	35411	35603	35793	35984
23	36173	36361	36549	36736	36922	37107	37291	37475	37658	37840
24	38021	38202	38382	38561	38739	38917	39094	39270	39445	39620
25	39794	39967	40140	40312	40483	40654	40824	40993	41162	41330
26	41497	41664	41830	41996	42160	42325	42488	42651	42813	42975
27	43136	43297	43457	43616	43775	43933	44091	44248	44404	44560
28	44716	44871	45025	45179	45332	45484	45637	45788	45939	46090
29	46240	46389	46538	46687	46835	46982	47129	47276	47422	47567
30	47712	47857	48001	48144	48287	48430	48572	48714	48855	48996
31	49136	49276	49415	49554	49693	49831	49969	50106	50243	50379
32	50515	50651	50786	50920	51055	51188	51322	51455	51587	51720
33	51851	51983	52114	52244	52375	52504	52634	52763	52892	53020
34	53148	53275	53403	53529	53656	53782	53908	54033	54158	54283
35	54407	54531	54654	54777	54900	55023	55145	55267	55388	55509
36	55630	55751	55871	55991	56110	56229	56348	56467	56585	56703
37	56820	56937	57054	57171	57287	57403	57519	57634	57749	57864
38	57978	58092	58206	58320	58433	58546	58659	58771	58883	58995
39	59106	59218	59329	59439	59550	59660	59770	59879	59988	60097
40	60206	60314	60423	60531	60638	60746	60853	60959	61066	61172
41	61278	61384	61490	61595	61700	61805	61909	62014	62118	62221
42	62325	62428	62531	62634	62737	62839	62941	63043	63144	63246

43	63347	63448	63548	63649	63749	63849	63949	64048	64147	64246
44	64345	64444	64542	64640	64738	64836	64933	65031	65128	65225
45	65321	65418	65514	65610	65706	65801	65896	65992	66087	66181
46	66276	66370	66464	66558	66652	66745	66839	66932	67025	67117
47	67210	67302	67394	67486	67578	67669	67761	67852	67943	68034
48	68124	68215	68305	68395	68485	68574	68664	68753	68842	68931
49	69020	69108	69197	69285	69373	69461	69548	69636	69723	69810
50	69897	69984	70070	70157	70243	70329	70415	70501	70586	70672
51	70757	70842	70927	71012	71096	71181	71265	71349	71433	71517
52	71600	71684	71767	71850	71933	72016	72099	72181	72263	72346
53	72428	72509	72591	72673	72754	72835	72916	72997	73078	73159
54	73239	73320	73400	73480	73560	73640	73719	73799	73878	73957
55	74036	74115	74194	74273	74351	74429	74507	74586	74663	74741
56	74819	74896	74974	75051	75128	75205	75282	75358	75435	75511
57	75587	75664	75740	75815	75891	75967	76042	76118	76193	76268
58	76343	76418	76492	76567	76641	76716	76790	76864	76938	77012
59	77085	77159	77232	77305	77379	77452	77525	77597	77670	77743
60	77815	77887	77960	78032	78104	78176	78247	78319	78390	78462
61	78533	78604	78675	78746	78817	78888	78958	79029	79099	79169
62	79239	79309	79379	79449	79518	79588	79657	79727	79796	79865
63	79934	80003	80072	80140	80209	80277	80346	80414	80482	80550
64	80618	80686	80754	80821	80889	80956	81023	81090	81158	81224
65	81291	81358	81425	81491	81558	81624	81690	81757	81823	81889
66	81954	82020	82086	82151	82217	82282	82347	82413	82478	82543
67	82607	82672	82737	82802	82866	82930	82995	83059	83123	83187
68	83251	83315	83378	83442	83506	83569	83632	83696	83759	83822
69	83885	83948	84011	84073	84136	84198	84261	84323	84386	84448
70	84510	84572	84634	84696	84757	84819	84880	84942	85003	85065
71	85126	85187	85248	85309	85370	85431	85491	85552	85612	85673
72	85733	85794	85854	85914	85974	86034	86094	86153	86213	86273
73	86332	86392	86451	86510	86570	86629	86688	86747	86806	86864
74	86923	86982	87040	87099	87157	87216	87274	87332	87390	87448
75	87506	87564	87622	87679	87737	87795	87852	87910	87967	88024
76	88081	88138	88195	88252	88309	88366	88423	88480	88536	88593
77	88649	88705	88762	88818	88874	88930	88986	89042	89098	89154
78	89209	89265	89321	89376	89432	89487	89542	89597	89653	89708
79	89763	89818	89873	89927	89982	90037	90091	90146	90200	90255

80	90309	90363	90417	90472	90526	90580	90634	90687	90741	90795
81	90849	90902	90956	91009	91062	91116	91169	91222	91275	91328
82	91381	91434	91487	91540	91593	91645	91698	91751	91803	91855
83	91908	91960	92012	92065	92117	92169	92221	92273	92324	92376
84	92428	92480	92531	92583	92634	92686	92737	92788	92840	92891
85	92942	92993	93044	93095	93146	93197	93247	93298	93349	93399
86	93450	93500	93551	93601	93651	93702	93752	93802	93852	93902
87	93952	94002	94052	94101	94151	94201	94250	94300	94349	94399
88	94448	94498	94547	94596	94645	94694	94743	94792	94841	94890
89	94939	94988	95036	95085	95134	95182	95231	95279	95328	95376
90	95424	95472	95521	95569	95617	95665	95713	95761	95809	95856
91	95904	95952	95999	96047	96095	96142	96190	96237	96284	96332
92	96379	96426	96473	96520	96567	96614	96661	96708	96755	96802
93	96848	96895	96942	96988	97035	97081	97128	97174	97220	97267
94	97313	97359	97405	97451	97497	97543	97589	97635	97681	97727
95	97772	97818	97864	97909	97955	98000	98046	98091	98137	98182
96	98227	98272	98318	98363	98408	98453	98498	98543	98588	98632
97	98677	98722	98767	98811	98856	98900	98945	98989	99034	99078
98	99123	99167	99211	99255	99300	99344	99388	99432	99476	99520
99	99564	99607	99651	99695	99739	99782	99826	99870	99913	99957

How to use the logarithmic table

A) The table contains two types of values, the logarithm argument **x**, in the first column, and the mantissas, in the other 10 columns. The five digits in the mantissas form the approximate value that comes after the dot, i. e., after the characteristic.

B) The logarithm arguments, in this table, have three digits, which are the two in the first column supplemented with the top figure of each of the ten columns of mantissas. In addition, the value in the first column has a implicit dot after the first place. So, to find, for example, log(1.34), we go to line 13 and look for the column under the figure 4, which is the fifth column of mantissas. We see the number 12710 there. So log(1.34) = 0.12710.

C) As the characteristic does not appear in the table, we write the logarithming in scientific notation (i. e., in notation of power of 10), so that this characteristic appears as an exponent. So, to find, for example, log(96300), we do log(96300) = = log(9.63*10^4) = log(9.63) + log(10^4) = 0.98363+4 = 4.98363.

D) The procedure is the same for positive logarithming less than 1. For example, to find log(0.0000452), we do: log(0.0000452) = log(4.52*10^{-5}) = 0.65514+(-5) = -4.34486.

E) To find the logarithming (logarithm argument) from a mantissa, just follow the opposite path to the one shown before. For example, mantissa 0.96237 is on line 91, under column 7. So the logarithming is 9.17, that is, log(9.17) = = 0.96237.

Test. Obtain from the table the value log(7290000). See example C above. The answer starts with 6 and ends with 3.

ANSWERS

P0.01) B) -16,   C) 10,   D) -11,   E) 5.
P0.02) B) +32, C) -15, D) +16, E) -28, F) -5.
P0.03) B) 89/60, C) 11/12, D) 131/84, E) 13/70, F) 17/20.
P0.04) B) 9/56, C) 4/15, D) 9/70, E) 1/4, F) 9/28
P0.05) B) 202, C) 92, D) 3, E) 18
P0.06) B) $(x^2-2y)/ax$, C) $(ay+b)/xy$, D) $(a^2+bc)/ab$, E) $(a^3-b^2c)/ac$
P0.07) B) 75%, D) 30%, D) 37.5%, E) 22.5%
P0.08) B) 37.5%, C) 50%, E) 60%, E) 62.5%
P0.09) B) 1.7, C) 0.8, D) 66.7, E) 1.5
P0.10) B) 0, C) 7, D) 29, E) 3
P0.11) B) 8.3333, C) 0.8889, D) 7.1429, E) 30.2436
P0.12) B) 833.33%, C) 88.89%, D) 714.29%, E) 3024.36%
P0.13) B) 22.22%, C) 9.09%, D) 57.14%, E) 8%
P0.14) B) \$15, C) \$42, D) 90 cm, E) 17.6 km
P0.15) B) \$168, C) \$57.50, D) \$288, E) \$303
P0.16) B) \$82.80, C) \$328, D) \$392, E) \$73.04
P0.17) B) 212.5%, C) 50%, D) 625%, E) 50%
P0.18) B) 80%, C) 45%, D) 20.59%, E) 14.29%
P0.19) B) 5.26%, C) 25%, D) 25%, E) 166.67%
P0.20) B) 15%, C) 52.5%, D) 14.29%, E) 12.5%
P0.21) B) 2, C) 5, D) 1, E) -1
P0.22) B) 96, C) 29, D) -64, E) 31
P0.23) B) 4, 62, C) 7, 102, D) 2, 35, E) 6, 93
P0.24) B) 2, C) 3, D) 5, E) 11/4
P0.25) B) 1720, C) 960, D) 936, E) 759
P0.26) B) 3, C) 1/2, D) -1, E) 3
P0.27) B) -10240, C) 3/2048, D) 708588, E) 2048
P0.28) B) (1/2, 5/4, 25/8, 125/16), C) (2, 10, 50, 250), D) (1, 1/3, 1/9, 1/27, 1/81), E) 3, 3/2, 3/4, 3/16)
P0.29) B) 3, C) 2, D) 4, E) 3
P0.30) B) 765, C) 21845, D) 510, E) 1640

P0.31) B) -42/5, C) 15/2, D) 5/2, E) 20

S0.01) -32, S0.02) a) 37/70, b) 64/45, S0.03) a) 3/35, b) 32/45, S0.04) 76, S0.05) a) $(15b - 2a^3)/3ab$, b) $(35b^2 + 2a^2)/10ab$, S0.06) a) 60%, b) 162.5%, c) 93.75%, S0.07) a) 0.47, b) 0.92, c) 0.03, d) 0.47, S0.08) a) 66.67%, b) 55.56%, c) 242.86%, d) 34.38%, S0.09) 13.33%, S0.10) a) $75, b) 8 m, c) 67.5 kg, S0.11) a) $228, b) $143.50, c) $362.50, S0.12) a) $352, b) $660, c) $291.20, S0.13) a) 60%, b) 33.33%, c) 33.33%, s0.14) a) 50%, b) 18.6%, c) 46.67%, S0.15) 12.5%, S0.16) a) 4, b) -2, c) 0, S0.17) 80, S0.18) a) 1, b) 2, S0.19) 4980, S0.20) a) 2, b) -1, c) 1/4, S0.21) 512, S0.22) 12, S0.24) 9

P1.01) B) 550 kg, C) 92 m^3, D) $94.50
P1.02) B) $96, C) $72, D) $180, E) $120
P1.03) B) $1296, C) $1272, D) $1380, E) $1320
P1.04) B) $150, C) $200, D) $790, E) $7660
P1.05) B) $225, $1225, C) $315, $2415, D) $2850, $12850, E) $144, $944
P1.06) B) $1960, C) $8550, D) $768, E) $1568
P1.07) B) 200 days, C) 40 days, D) 280 days, E) 100 days
P1.08) B) 9.36 m, C) 21.632 m, D) 94.488576 cm, E) 2.33971712 m
P1.09) B) $1,144,44, C) $1,591.41, D) $378.85, E) $10,400
P1.10) B) 6,494.59, C) 6,365.40, D) $7,293.04
P1.11) B) $364.65, C) $938.24, D) $1,061.36, E) $974.19
P1.12) B) $1,153.40, C) $1,109.47, D) $1,068.00, E) $1,176.36
P1.13) B) 22.47%, C) 41.42%, D) 11.8%, E) 93.65%

S1.01) 2.499 m, 124.97%, S1.02) $176, $376, S1.03) $330, $3,330, S1.04) $5,840, S1.05) 125 days, S1.06) 6.1208%, S1.07) 6.1208%, 0.41616 m, S1.08) $10,927.27, S1.09) $10,528.73, S1.10) $7,549.94, S1.11) 2.5% p.m.

P2.01) B) 2, 4, 8, C) 4, 16, 64, D) 1/2, 1/4, 1/8, E) 3/2, 9/4,

27/8

P2.02) B) 1/2, 1, 2: increasing, C) 1/3, 1, 3: increasing, D) 2, 1, 1/2: decreasing, E) 3/4, 1, 4/3: increasing

P2.03) B) -8, C) 4, D) 5/2, E) 4, 5

P2.04) B) 5, C) 2, D) 3, E) -3

P2.05) B) log4, C) log77, D) log5, E) log3

P2.06) B) 2, C) 3, D) 8, E) 6

P2.07) B) log11/log5, C) log3/log2, D) log2/log7, E) log19/log3

P2.08) B) 1.54407, C) 1.17609, D) 1.80618, E) 1.32222, F) 1.90848

P2.09) B) 84510/95424, C) 84510/30103, D) 47712/69897, E) 95424/60206

P2.10) B) 0.52288, C) -0.84510, D) 1.04576, E) -0.39794, F) -1.47712

P2.11) B) -0.14509, C) 1.67394, D) -2.63827, E) 4.91908

P2.12) B) 35, C) 11 (ceiling for 10.36), D) 23, E) 24

P2.13) B) 18, C) 12 (ceiling for 11.27), D) 24, E) 136

P2.14) B) 6.5% (from the average between 1.06 and 1.07), C) 3%, D) 1%

P2.15) B) 11.11%, C) 9.52%, D) 16.65%, E) 9.84%

P2.16) B) 17.04%, C) 5.57%, D) 16.48%, E) 16.70%

P2.17) B) 0.1998%, C) 5.83%, D) 0.07997%, E) 9.53%

P2.18) B) $1,100.01, C) $1,777.99, D) $1,600.19, E) $1,070.00

P2.19) B) $1,771.73, C) $1,879.84, D) $1,472.32, E) $2,235.43

P2.20) B) $3,443.30 equal, C) $3,471.58 bigger, D) $4,329.34 bigger, E) $3,386.75 smaller

S2.01) 1/5, 1/25, 1/625, S2.02) $20,000, 3%, S2.03) x=2, S2.04) a) 6, b) 4, c) -1, 2.05) a) log12, b) log3, c) log4, S2.06) a) 5, b) 2, c) 2, S2.07) a) log7/log5, b) log3/log11, c) log12/log13, d) log2/log3, S2.08) a) 0.77815, b) 1.07918, c) 1.65321, d) 1.38021, S2.09) a) 84510/47712, b) 84510/69897, c) 69897/30103, d) 47712/104139, S2.10) a) -0.52288, b) 0.14613. c) 0.22185, d) -0.10914, S2.11) a) -2.44855, b) 4.93146, c) -1.82681, d) 6.97405, S2.12) 8 (ceiling for 7.3),

S2.13) 7 (ceiling for 6.7), S2.14) 3.7%, S2.15) 1.85%, S2.16) 12.32%, S2.17) 1.98%, S2.18) \$5,089.39, S2.19) \$172.34, S2.20) A: \$50.30, B: \$254.60, advantage in the bank B

P3.01) B) \$567.73, C) \$676.72, D) \$504.65, E) \$747.55
P3.02) B) \$556.60, C) \$670.02, D) \$494.75, E) \$736.50
P3.03) B) \$1,268.25, C) \$1,480.27, D) \$1,850.33, E) \$2,536.50
P3.04) B) \$1,125.51, C) \$1,394.27, D) \$1,742.84, E) \$2,251.02
P3.05) B) P = \$879.06, A = \$7,029.96, C) P = \$1,796.62, A = = \$2,023.88, D) P = \$2,295.50, A = \$2,485.70, E) P = = \$1,197.75, A = \$1,349.25
P3.06) B) \$1,214.25, C) \$933,89, D) \$1,664.84, E) \$1,042.84

S3.01) \$2,123.65, S3.02) A = \$4,291.48, P = \$3,662.74, S3.03) \$2,744.44, S3.04) \$2,673.87, S3.05) \$1,789.35, S3.06) \$870.29

P4.01) B) \$100, C) \$80, D) \$120, E) \$200
P4.02) B) \$100, C) \$180, D) \$300, E) \$140
P4.03) B) 0.0973, C) 0.0886, D) 0.0961, E) 0.1027
P4.04) B) 15 months, C) 11 months, D) 16 months, E) 17 months
P4.05) B) 15 months, C) 13 months, D) 16 months, E) 12 months
P4.06) B) \$1,226.76, C) \$1,846.64, D) \$1,674.06, E) \$2,097.91

S4.01) \$79.75, S4.02) \$130, S4.03) \$295.82 (P = \$566.04), S4.04) 20 months, S4.05) i between (1/4)% and (1/3)%, j between 3% and 4%.

P5.01) B) \$805.26, C) \$931.06, D) \$3,464.76, E) \$922.82
P5.02) (We show here the last period)

Period	(a=a'-d')	(b=a*i)	(c=R)	(d=c-b)
B)	5	1609.59	4.83	1614.43	1609.60
C)	5	2027.97	14.20	2042.20	2028.00
D)	5	1219.21	9.75	1228.95	1219.20

E) 5   1003.99   2.01   1006.01   1004.00

P5.03) B) s = \$4.814.38, e = \$3.185.62, C) s = \$6,041.82,
   e = \$3,958.18, D) s = \$3,628.64, e = \$2,371.36,
   E) s = \$3,006.97, e = \$1,993.03

P5.04) (We show here the last period)

Period	$a=d'*i$	$b=R$	$c=a+b$	$d=d'+c$
B) 6	33.27	1650.08	1683.35	10000.02
Total:	99.54	9900.48	10000.02, $A*j+R$ = 1675.08	
C) 6	16.63	825.04	841.67	5000.00
Total:	49.76	4950.24	5000.01, $A*j+R$ = 847.54	
D) 6	19.96	990.05	1010.01	6000.03
Total:	59.73	5940.30	6000.03. $A*j+R$ = 1008.05	
E) 6	31.60	1567.57	1599.17	9500.08
Total:	9.56	9405.42	9499.98, $A*j+R$ = 1586.57	

P5.05) (We show here the last period)

n	$[a=C(1-i)^n]$	$(b = a'-a)$	$(c = c'+b)$
B) 6	806.74	320.38	5193.26
C) 6	1500.00	522.01	7500.00
D) 6	1100.00	514.58	9900.00
E) 6	2000.00	615.32	8000.00

P5.06) (We show here the last period)

n (a=R) (b=d'*i) (c=a+b) (d=d'+c) (e=e'-c)

B) 5 1690.99 139.39 1830.38 8799.98 1200.02; R = 1690.99
C) 5 1843.27 313.10 2156.37 9983.75 1016.25; R = 1843.27
D) 5 3074.53 253.44 3327.97 15999.98 2000.02: R = 3074.53
E) 5 4756.17 493.75 5249.92 24999.98 5000.02; R = 4756.17

P5.07) B) \$1,239,598.35, C) \$1,071,609.27, D) \$1,573,485.69,
E) \$292,162.96

P5.08) B) V = \$788.93, F = \$814.54, C) V = \$1,089.09, F =
= \$1,113.29, D) V = \$1,261.89, F = \$1,346.42, E) V = \$878.82,
F = \$927.44

P5.09) B) V = \$3,532.50, A = \$3,042.37, C) V = \$1,387.89, A =
= \$1,685.10, D) V = \$1,917.87, A = \$2,011.98, E) V = \$2,875.78,
A = \$3,068.41

P5.10) B) \$166.67, C) \$387.50, D) \$285.71, E) \$313.33

P5.11) B) \$115,309.34, C) \$152,225.31, D) \$253,070.00, E) \$221,652.24

S5.01) R = \$573.69
S5.02) R = \$423.69
    (We show here the last period)

n	(a=a'-d')	(b=a*i)	(c=R)	(d=c-b)
6	421.87	2.11	423.99	421.88

S5.03) (We show here the last period)

n	(a=d'*i)	(b=R)	(c=a+b)	(d=d'+c)
5	25.14	1387.46	1412.60	7000.16

Total: 62.76 6937.30   7000.16 ---; A*j+R = 1415.46

S5.04) (We show here the last period)

n	$(a=C(1-i)^n)$	(b = a'-a)	(c = c'+b)
5	1000.00	551.85	8000.00

S5.05) (We show here the last period)
R = 256.30

n	(a=R)	(b=d'*i)	(c=a+b)	(d=d'+c)	(e=e'-c)
6	256.30	55.53	312.03	1700.22	18299.78

        d+e = 20000.00

S5.06) V = \$1,104.51, F = \$1,140.35, S5.07) R = \$250.75, S5.08) P = \$2,145.82, A = \$2.227,71, S5.09) P = \$383,33, S5.10) C = \$90.422,88

P6.01) B) C = \$9,956.53, C) C = \$11,561.36, D) C = \$11,081.17, E) C = \$10,186.52
P6.02) B) F = \$11,006.20; V = \$11,446.45, C) F = \$9,996.94; V = \$1,0396.81, D) F = \$10,978.21; V = \$11,417.34, E) F = = \$10,107.29; V = \$10,511.58
P6.03) B) \$12,434.01, C) \$38.837.41, D) \$41,474.84, E) \$28,003.10

S6.01) \$4,357.70, S6.02) \$9,535.44, S6.03) \$4,944.55, S6.04) \$8,763.89, S6.05) \$9,639.64, S6.06) \$13,445.62

@cacildo